SPECTRUM®

Language Arts

Grade 7

Published by Spectrum®
an imprint of Carson Dellosa Education
Greensboro, NC

Spectrum®
An imprint of Carson Dellosa Education
PO Box 35665
Greensboro, NC 27425 USA

ISBN 978-1-4838-1211-3

02-086207784

Chapter 1 Grammar
Parts of Speech

Lesson 1.1 Common and Proper Nouns 5
Lesson 1.2 Collective and Abstract Nouns 7
Lesson 1.3 Plurals and Possessives 9
Lesson 1.4 Appositives 11
Lesson 1.5 Personal Pronouns 13
Lesson 1.6 Intensive and Reflexive Pronouns 15
Lesson 1.7 Indefinite Pronouns 17
Lesson 1.8 Pronoun Shifts 19
Review: Lessons 1.1–1.8 21

Lesson 1.9 Action Verbs 23
Lesson 1.10 Subject-Verb Agreement 25
Lesson 1.11 Transitive and Intransitive Verbs 27
Lesson 1.12 Helping and Linking Verbs 29
Lesson 1.13 Gerunds, Participles, and Infinitives 31
Lesson 1.14 Verb Tenses 33
Lesson 1.15 Verb Tenses: Progressive 35
Lesson 1.16 Verb Tenses: Perfect 37
Review: Lessons 1.9–1.16 39

Lesson 1.17 Adjectives and Predicate Adjectives 41
Lesson 1.18 Comparative and Superlative Adjectives 43
Lesson 1.19 Adverbs and Intensifiers 45
Lesson 1.20 Comparative and Superlative Adverbs 47
Lesson 1.21 Adjectives and Adverbs 49
Lesson 1.22 Prepositions and Prepositional Phrases 51
Lesson 1.23 Conjunctions and Interjections 53
Review: Lessons 1.17–1.23 55

Sentences

Lesson 1.24 Sentence Types 57
Lesson 1.25 Simple and Compound Sentences 59
Lesson 1.26 Complex Sentences 61
Lesson 1.27 Adjective and Adverb Clauses 63
Review: Lessons 1.24–1.27 65

Chapter 2 Mechanics

Lesson 2.1 Capitalization: Sentences, Quotations, Letter Parts 67
Lesson 2.2 Capitalization: Names, Titles, and Places 69
Lesson 2.3 Capitalization: Other Proper Nouns 71
Lesson 2.4 End Marks 73
Review: Lessons 2.1–2.4 75

Lesson 2.5 Commas: Series, Direct Address, Multiple Adjectives 77
Lesson 2.6 Commas: Combining Sentences, Setting Off Dialogue 79
Lesson 2.7 Commas: Personal Letters and Business Letters 81
Lesson 2.8 Semicolons and Colons 83
Lesson 2.9 Quotation Marks 85
Lesson 2.10 Using Italics and Underlining 87
Lesson 2.11 Apostrophes 89
Lesson 2.12 Hyphens, Dashes, and Parentheses 91
Review: Lessons 2.5–2.12 93

Chapter 3 Usage

Lesson 3.1 Word Roots 95
Lesson 3.2 Prefixes and Suffixes 97
Lesson 3.3 Double Negatives 101
Lesson 3.4 Synonyms and Antonyms 103
Lesson 3.5 Analogies 105
Review: Lessons 3.1–3.5 107

Lesson 3.6 Homophones 109
Lesson 3.7 Multiple-Meaning Words 111
Lesson 3.8 Connotations and Denotations 113
Lesson 3.9 Figures of Speech: Similes, Metaphors, and Personification 115
Review: Lessons 3.6–3.9 119

Chapter 4 Writer's Guide

Lesson 4.1 Prewriting 121
Lesson 4.2 Drafting 122
Lesson 4.3 Revising 123
Lesson 4.4 Proofreading 124
Lesson 4.5 Publishing 125
Lesson 4.6 Evaluating Writing 126
Lesson 4.7 Writing Process Practice 127

Answer Key 132

Chapter 1 Grammar

Lesson 1.1 Common and Proper Nouns

Common nouns name people, places, things, and ideas.

> People: butcher, nephew, landscaper, jogger, teenager, pilot
> Places: home, ice cream shop, college, bookstore, basement
> Things: violet, floor, photograph, pond, mercury, government
> Ideas: happiness, freedom, anxiety, enthusiasm, truth

Proper nouns name specific people, places, and things. Proper nouns are capitalized.

> People: Charlie, Mr. Rodriguez, Dr. Chang, Officer Bates
> Places: Tijuana, Yellowstone National Park, Virginia
> Things: Tasty Time Pizza, the Iron Age

Identify It

Underline the common noun(s) and circle the proper noun(s) in each sentence.

1. Most people consider the Home Insurance Building to be the first skyscraper.

2. It was built in Chicago in 1884 and rose to a height of ten stories.

3. Others think the Jayne Building in Philadelphia should have the honor.

4. For nearly 40 years, the Empire State Building in New York City was the tallest building on Earth.

5. The World Trade Center held the record for two years, but then the Sears Tower was completed.

6. The Sears Tower, known today as Willis Tower, was overtaken by the Petronas Towers in Kuala Lumpur, the capital of Malaysia.

7. Taipei 101 in Taiwan was the first building to exceed 500 meters in height.

8. The tallest skyscraper in the world is the Burj Khalifa in the city of Dubai.

Lesson 1.1 Common and Proper Nouns

Proof It

Correct the mistakes in the use of common and proper nouns using proofreading marks.

| / – lowercase letter |
| ≡ – capitalize letter |

1. We are going to visit grandpa Mick in Tampa bay, Florida, next Week.

2. My Brother Tim plans to bring along his fishing pole and tackle box.

3. He and Grandpa will drive to lake Harris on monday to catch Trout and Catfish.

4. On Tuesday, my Mom and Dad are riding their Mountain Bikes on wilkin's swamp trail.

5. I'm looking forward to Wednesday Afternoon, when we will be heading to ronnie's reptile world to see the alligators.

6. My grandpa loves listening to old frank sinatra records while he dances around the Living Room.

7. As soon as we get home, I have to finish writing my Report about the declaration of independence.

8. Mr. Woodlock is my History Teacher at Broughten jr. high school.

Try It

Write a paragraph about your favorite book or movie. Use at least six common and six proper nouns correctly.

My favorite movie is We Bare Bears: The Movie. Some of my favorite part(s) is when they fight the antagonist on the helicopter. The weirdest part is when the bears naturally join society. The funniest part for me is the beginning where they hack every single electron ic and do some interesting stuff, after the whole city has a power-outtage, also another weird part, they find a bunch of litteral party animal influencer group

Lesson 1.2 Collective and Abstract Nouns

Collective nouns are used to describe groups of specific animals, people, or things.

> A group of horses is a *herd.*
> A group of students is a *class.*
> A group of mountains is a *range.*

A collective noun refers to more than one thing, but it acts as a singular noun when used in a sentence.

> Incorrect: The *herd are* running back to the barn.
> Correct: The *herd is* running back to the barn.

Abstract nouns describe ideas rather than people, places, or things that can be perceived with the five senses.

courage   laziness   information   beauty   hate

Match It

Match each plural noun in the left column with its singular collective noun in the right column.

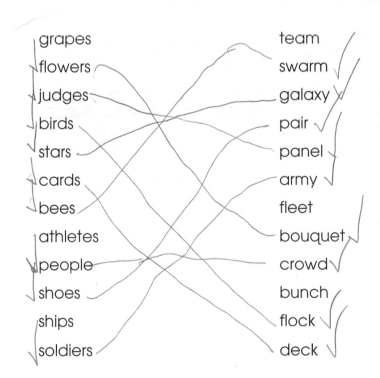

grapes	team
flowers	swarm
judges	galaxy
birds	pair
stars	panel
cards	army
bees	fleet
athletes	bouquet
people	crowd
shoes	bunch
ships	flock
soldiers	deck

Lesson 1.2 Collective and Abstract Nouns

Complete It

Circle the verb in each sentence that correctly completes the sentence.

1. The staff (is, are) getting the day off work because of a holiday.

2. A pride of lions (stalk, stalks) the savannah in search of food.

3. Courageousness (mean, means) feeling scared but taking action anyway.

4. The entire neighborhood (attend, attends) the annual block party.

5. The dance troupe (perform, performs) three shows each Saturday this month.

6. The crew (prepare, prepares) the ship for its long journey to the South Seas.

7. A choir (sing, sings) at the mall during the Christmas season.

8. The fleet (sail, sails) from San Francisco to Honolulu and back again each spring.

9. My family (is, are) volunteering at the food pantry this weekend.

10. Beth's singing ability (enable, enables) her to join any chorus she chooses.

11. The audience (cheer, cheers) as the magician grabs a scarf out of a puff of smoke.

12. A team of horses (pull, pulls) the wagon across a desolate, frozen prairie.

Try It

For each abstract noun, write a sentence that uses it correctly. If you are unsure of a noun's meaning, use a dictionary to find its definition.

success	justice	misery	anger	parenthood
leisure	compassion	friendship	loyalty	curiosity

_____

_____

_____

_____

_____

_____

_____

_____

_____

Lesson 1.3 Plurals and Possessives

Although **plural** and **possessive nouns** often sound similar, they are spelled differently and have different meanings.

Plural noun: The *bats* roost deep within the cave.
Singular possessive noun: The *bat's* roost is located deep within the cave.
Plural possessive noun: The *bats'* roost is located deep within the cave.

Rewrite It
Rewrite each sentence to correct the word in bold.

1. **Cave's** are not the only places where bats roost.

_____

2. These flying **mammals** homes are also found beneath bridges and inside hollow trees.

_____

3. **Predators'** don't think to look for bats in these out-of-the-way places.

_____

4. Bats cluster together in **colony's** because it keeps them warm and safe.

_____

5. Unlike birds, **bats** wings are not strong enough to lift them from the ground and into the air.

_____

6. A **bats'** hind legs are also weak, so they cannot get a running start.

_____

7. Instead, bats use their **claws'** to climb to a high place.

_____

8. The **claw's** grip the surface, and the bat relaxes.

_____

9. **Gravities** pull locks the claws—and the bat—in place.

_____

10. The **bats'** muscles do not need to exert any energy.

_____

Lesson 1.3 Plurals and Possessives

Identify It
Look at the boldface word in each sentence. On the line, write **PL** if the word is a plural noun, **SP** if the word is a singular possessive, and **PP** if the word is a plural possessive.

1. _____ The **paleontologists** flew to Montana to hunt for fossils.

2. _____ **Dr. Harris's** plane touched down on a grassy runway in the middle of nowhere.

3. _____ As the plane bounced along, the **scientists'** equipment rattled around inside steel boxes.

4. _____ The steep, rocky **sides** of a mountain towered over the flat valley.

5. _____ A local **rancher's** pickup waited near the runway.

6. _____ The truck would carry the **boxes** of equipment to the dig site.

7. _____ Dr. Gupta drove the truck across the **valley's** bumpy landscape.

8. _____ **Clouds'** shadows moved slowly over the distant mountain.

9. _____ An hour later, the scientists arrived at the **mountain's** base.

10. _____ A camp had been set up, with several **tents** encircling a large fire pit.

11. _____ The excavation **site's** location was within walking distance of the camp.

12. _____ The **doctors'** excitement was easy to see; they both had huge grins on their faces!

Try It
Write three sentences, each using one of the words below. Each sentence will use a different word.

| dinosaurs | dinosaur's | dinosaurs' |

1. _____

_____

2. _____

_____

3. _____

_____

Lesson 1.4 Appositives

An **appositive** is a noun or phrase that renames another noun in a sentence. The appositive offers more information about the noun.

> Harriet, a golden retriever, has been my constant companion since she was a puppy.
> The phrase *a golden retriever* is an appositive that renames *Harriet*.

When the appositive is non-essential, or not necessary to the sentence, it should have a comma before and after it. In the example above, you can remove the appositive and the sentence still makes sense.

Identify It

Read each sentence below. Underline the appositives. Circle the nouns they rename.

1. The Windsor Pumpkin Regatta, a water race in Nova Scotia, was begun in 1999.

2. Danny Dill, the founder of the race, is the son of a breeder of giant pumpkins.

3. Contestants, who must paddle half a mile, use giant hollowed-out pumpkins as small watercraft.

4. The regatta, the first of its kind, has inspired other races around North America.

5. The first step in creating pumpkin boats is to hollow out giant pumpkins, some of which weigh 700 pounds!

6. The pumpkin, which rots relatively quickly, needs to be hollowed up just a day or two before the race.

7. A pumpkin boat, also known as a personal vegetable craft (PVC), is not easy to navigate.

8. Leo Swinamer, a nine-time winner of the regatta, is in his mid-seventies!

9. The race, which has three classes, is attended by thousands of spectators every year.

10. The first person to use a pumpkin as a boat was Wayne Hackney, a pumpkin farmer from New Hampshire.

Lesson 1.4 Appositives

Proof It

Read the paragraph below. It contains five appositives that are missing commas. Use this proofreading symbol ⌄ to add commas where they are needed.

Pumpkins a type of squash are a symbol of fall to many people. These large ribbed fruits are round in shape, heavy, and filled with seeds. Pumpkin vines which wind their way through pumpkin patches can be covered in small prickly hairs. This can make picking a little irritating! In recent years, pick-your-own pumpkin patches have increased in popularity. Many families enjoy the tradition of a yearly trip to the patch. Pumpkins which are often carved at Halloween also have many other uses. Many people like to eat pumpkin pie a tradition at Thanksgiving. Pumpkin muffins, bread, and cheesecake also have their fans. Although most people use pureed pumpkin, the flowers, seeds, and leaves are also edible. The seeds a delicious snack when roasted can be a healthy, nutritious treat.

Try It

Write four sentences on the lines below. Each one should contain an appositive. Remember to punctuate the appositives correctly.

1. _____

_____

2. _____

_____

3. _____

_____

4. _____

_____

Lesson 1.5 Personal Pronouns

A **pronoun** is a word used in place of a noun. A **subject pronoun** can be used as the subject of a sentence. It can be singular (*I, you, he, she, it*) or plural (*we, you, they*).

She hoped that Uncle Ralph would visit on Sunday.

An **object pronoun** is the object of a verb or a preposition. It can also be singular (*me, you, him, her, it*) or plural (*us, you, them*).

Clare wanted *us* to go to the concert tomorrow night.

A **possessive pronoun** shows possession. Singular possessive pronouns are *my, mine, your, yours, his, her, hers,* and *its,* and plural possessive pronouns are *our, ours, your, yours, their,* and *theirs.*

Their sprinkler has been on for three hours.

Identify It

Read each sentence below and decide how the **boldface** pronoun is used. On the line, write **SP** for subject pronoun, **OP** for object pronoun, or **PP** for possessive pronoun.

1. _____ Kembe and **his** dad like to explore caves together.

2. _____ **They** first started spelunking, or caving, when Kembe was twelve.

3. _____ Kembe's parents gave **him** some gear as an early birthday present.

4. _____ "**We** really hope that you enjoy caving," said Kembe's parents as he unwrapped a headlamp.

5. _____ "It has given **me** a real appreciation for the beauty of the natural world," added Mr. Ly.

6. _____ Kembe and his dad have traveled to sixteen different states to pursue **their** hobby, but Kembe's mom prefers to stay home.

7. _____ She has claustrophobia, and tight places make **her** uncomfortable.

8. _____ **She** has a hard time understanding why Kembe and Mr. Ly love exploring underground.

9. _____ "**It** is hard to explain," Mr. Ly admits.

10. _____ "**Our** trips to explore hidden places are just so exciting!" adds Kembe.

Lesson 1.5 Personal Pronouns

Complete It

Read the passage below. Circle the correct pronoun from each pair in parentheses.

Have (you, we) ever visited Linville Caverns in the mountains of western North Carolina? If you are ever in the area, (its, it) is definitely worth a trip. (Their, Your) guide is likely to tell the group about two teenage boys who explored the caverns on (our, their) own in the early 1900s. The duo was not dressed for the cool 52-degree temperature of the caverns. They eagerly explored the caves with only a lantern to guide (them, him) through the pitch–dark maze. Today, visitors tread on comfortable walkways, and ropes guide them away from the chilly underground stream. This wasn't always the case, though, and the foolish boys were unprepared for the rocky paths.

At one point, the boy holding the lantern dropped and broke (its, it). He and (his, her) partner were left in such darkness that (their, they) could not see their own hands six inches from (their, our) faces! Can (us, you) imagine the panic you'd feel? Luckily, the boys discovered that if they put their hands in the stream, they could detect which way (he, it) flowed. (Them, They) knew that it eventually flowed out of the caverns, so they would need to move in the direction the water was flowing. It took (him, them) two days, but they finally traveled the 800 feet to the cave's entrance. They had hypothermia, and it took them a while to recover, but the boys were lucky to have lived to tell the tale!

Try It

Write several sentences about a place you've explored. Circle each pronoun you use.

_____

_____

_____

_____

_____

Lesson 1.6 Intensive and Reflexive Pronouns

Intensive and **reflexive pronouns** are pronouns that end in *–self* or *–selves*. The way the pronoun is used determines whether it is intensive or reflexive.

Intensive pronouns usually appear right after the subject of a sentence. They emphasize the subject.

> I *myself* am planning to run the 5K on New Year's Day.
> She *herself* is going to repaint the entire interior of the house.

Reflexive pronouns appear elsewhere in the sentence and refer back to the subject.

> The rabbit scratched *itself* and then hopped into the garden.
> We gave *ourselves* a few extra minutes to get ready before the performance.

Complete It
Complete each sentence below with a reflexive or an intensive pronoun.

1. I _____ have never visited a library I didn't love.

2. Kaylie gave _____ a haircut when she was only three, and her mother was not pleased.

3. You and Elijah can make the pizza dough _____ if you have enough time.

4. Jackson read to _____ all afternoon, and then he took a nap.

5. They _____ weren't sure what was going on when the tornado touched down.

6. The team captain _____ gave a speech after the final game of the season.

7. I asked _____ over and over again if I had made the right decision.

8. The teacher _____ bought most of the books on the shelf in the classroom.

9. My father used to tell me that if I wanted to succeed in life, I needed to believe in _____.

10. My grandparents _____ took care of all the crops and all the animals on the farm.

Lesson 1.6 Intensive and Reflexive Pronouns

Identify It

In each sentence below, the intensive or reflexive pronoun is boldface. Underline the subject the pronoun refers to.

1. The day before the yard sale, Henry **himself** moved fourteen boxes out of the attic.

2. His younger brother and sister helped **themselves** to the things that they felt attached to.

3. There was an old wooden wagon that Mr. Waxhaw **himself** had used when he was first learning how to walk.

4. One box contained quilts that Henry's grandmother had made **herself**.

5. On the day of the sale, it was hot outside, but the attic **itself** was sweltering.

6. June and Xander, Henry's siblings, sprayed **themselves** with a water bottle to keep cool.

7. "Did you **yourself** collect all these cards?" a customer asked Henry, pointing to a collection of baseball cards.

8. "I'm actually not that interested in baseball **myself**," replied Henry. "They were my uncle's cards."

9. At the end of the day, Henry's parents congratulated **themselves** on a clean attic.

10. "We should treat **ourselves** to dinner out with the money we earned!" suggested Mr. Waxhaw.

Try It

Write four sentences using intensive and reflexive pronouns. Circle the intensive pronouns and underline the reflexive pronouns.

1. _____

_____

2. _____

_____

3. _____

_____

4. _____

_____

Lesson 1.7 Indefinite Pronouns

Indefinite pronouns are pronouns that do not specifically name the noun that comes before it.

> another anybody anyone anything each everybody everyone
> everything nobody none no one nothing one somebody someone

> I handed my keys to *someone* behind the counter.
> *Each* of my relatives has dark hair.
> *Everyone* leaves through the door on the right.

Most indefinite pronouns are singular, but the following are plural:

> both few many others several

> *Several* of the books were donated to the library.
> *Few* visit the zoo on days when it is pouring rain.

Some indefinite pronouns, such as *all, any, more, most,* and *some,* are either singular or plural, depending on their meaning in the sentence.

> *All* is revealed at the end of the book.
> *All* of the children are coming to the party.

Identify It
Underline the indefinite pronoun in each sentence.

1. Everybody loves vacationing at the beach, right?

2. If there is anything troubling you, Shawna, let me know.

3. Keith knocked at the door, but nobody answered.

4. Somebody left a note about finding a lost dog in the park.

5. When Lani got to school, the doors were locked because no one else had arrived yet.

6. The free samples of lotion had already been taken by others, so I went home empty-handed.

7. All of the trees in that lot were chopped down last fall.

8. Both of the kittens pounced at the string.

9. Rex didn't want any, so he politely said, "No, thank you."

10. When the band finally came onstage at midnight, many had already gone home.

Lesson 1.7 Indefinite Pronouns

Complete It
Complete each sentence by circling the correct form of the verb shown in parentheses.

1. When everybody (leave, leaves) tonight, please make sure you turn out the lights.

2. All of us (need, needs) to be aware of how much energy we use.

3. Nothing (is, are) as hard to imagine as a world without oil or coal.

4. However, both (is, are) nonrenewable resources.

5. Until somebody (discover, discovers) a free, unlimited energy source, we will need to be careful about the energy we use.

6. Everyone (has, have) a responsibility to take care of our planet.

7. Today, few (disagree, disagrees) with the idea that wind power and solar power are cleaner energy options.

8. Either (create, creates) energy with less pollution than coal or oil.

9. Neither (is, are) a perfect solution, but each (is, are) a better option than using fossil fuels.

Try It
Choose four indefinite pronouns, and write a sentence using each. At the end of each sentence, write **S** if the pronoun is singular and **P** if it is plural.

1. _____

_____

2. _____

_____

3. _____

_____

4. _____

_____

Lesson 1.8 Pronoun Shifts

A **pronoun shift** happens when a writer changes pronouns in the middle of a sentence or paragraph. This can confuse the reader.

In this example, the writer changes from *they* (third-person plural) to *you* (second-person singular):

Incorrect: When people visit the Statue of Liberty, *they* are often disappointed to learn that *you* are not allowed to walk all the way up to the torch.

Correct: When people visit the Statue of Liberty, *they* are often disappointed to learn that *they* cannot walk all the way up to the torch.

In this example, there is no agreement between *fences* (a plural noun) and *it* (third-person singular pronoun).

Incorrect: The farmer built tall *fences* around his fields because *it* will help keep deer from eating his crops.

Correct: The farmer built tall *fences* around his fields because *they* will help keep deer from eating his crops.

Proof It
Rewrite each sentence to correct the pronoun shift.

1. A professional pianist must practice every day if they want to succeed.

_____

2. A child under the age of 13 needs to be accompanied by their parents.

_____

3. Linh and Sammi invited us to go with her to the movies.

_____

4. Scientists understand that even when an experiment fails, you can still learn something.

_____

5. A patient surfer will wait for just the right wave before they stand up and ride to shore.

_____

6. Most students understand that studying hard will help you get good grades.

_____

Lesson 1.8 Pronoun Shifts

Complete It
Circle the pronoun that correctly completes the sentence.

1. The committee met last night, and (it, they) decided to approve the new soccer field.

2. When my brother and I got home, (he, we) made sandwiches together.

3. Grace and Jacob were nervous because (we, they) had never performed in front of a crowd.

4. After the storm, earthworms emerged from the ground, and (it, they) began crawling across the sidewalk.

5. If a student must wait for the bus in the dark, be sure to give (him or her, them) a flashlight.

6. A new chef faces challenges, but with hard work, (she, you) can become successful.

7. The movers struggled to get the piano up the stairs, but at last (we, they) got the piano into the music room.

8. After two years, construction for the new garden center was completed last week, and (it, they) will finally open on Saturday.

9. The words in the book were printed very small, but I could still read (it, them).

10. When people order pizza by phone, (you, they) can choose to have the pizza delivered or go pick it up.

11. When singers join this choir, (you, they) will often get to perform in different places around the city.

12. Many people go on vacation in August because the weather is nice and (their, your) kids don't have to be back in school yet.

Try It
On the lines below, write a short description about a place you would like to visit, including what the experience would be like. Circle each pronoun you use, and proofread your paragraph to be sure there are no pronoun shifts.

_____

_____

_____

_____

_____

Review: Common and Proper Nouns, Collective and Abstract Nouns, Plurals and Possessives, Appositives

Identify the underlined word using the key in the box. Write your answer on the line following each underlined word.

a. common noun	b. proper noun	c. collective noun	d. abstract noun

1. Desmond's <u>family</u> _____ moved to <u>Cleveland</u> _____, Ohio, when Mrs. Otto took a job with <u>NASA</u> _____.

2. One of <u>Becca's</u> _____ favorite memories of her <u>childhood</u> _____ is visiting <u>relatives</u> _____ in <u>Spain</u> _____ and befriending a <u>colony</u> _____ of cats that lived near the <u>wharf</u> _____ in a seaside town.

3. Chloe opened the <u>Sweet Tooth Bake Shop</u> _____ last <u>April</u> _____ because she loves to see the <u>delight</u> _____ and <u>pleasure</u> _____ on children's faces when they get to choose a treat.

4. In her carry-on <u>bag</u> _____, Ms. Tanaka packed a book, a <u>pack</u> _____ of cards, an overnight kit, one outfit, and an extra <u>pair</u> _____ of shoes.

In the sentences below, circle singular possessives, underline plurals, and underline plural possessives twice.

1. Mr. Gillingham's students are entering their science projects in a citywide science fair.

2. The students' parents will drive them to the auditorium downtown.

3. Ryan's project, a 3D model of the sun, took him two weeks to construct.

4. The Wong twins' volcano produces lava and spews tiny rocks.

5. The project we think will win shows how different kinds of stress affect people's bodies.

One sentence above contains an appositive. Write the appositive on the line below.

_____

Review Chapter 1 Lessons 1-8

Review: Personal Pronouns, Intensive and Reflexive Pronouns, Indefinite Pronouns, Pronoun Shifts

Underline the word that best completes each sentence below.

1. Although Jane and Gabriela are best friends, (them, they) do have frequent disagreements.

2. I (myself, yourself) do not enjoy watching scary movies at all.

3. The students who are going to France this summer must work on their French if (you, they) hope to be understood.

4. Morgan and Matt decided that they would throw a surprise birthday party for (them, their) little sister.

5. Mom decided to treat (herself, itself) to a movie and a cup of coffee with (she, her) sister.

6. Uncle Zach and (me, I) are going to stop at the grocery store before (we, they) start dinner.

7. Each of the giraffes cautiously (visit, visits) the watering hole for a drink.

8. When your sisters arrive at the party, tell (them, her) to call me.

9. Micah (itself, himself) will be delivering the gift boxes to all his customers.

10. Both the principal and the vice principal (think, thinks) that students should attend school year-round.

Identify the underlined pronoun in each sentence as a subject pronoun (**SP**), object pronoun (**OP**), or possessive pronoun (**PP**).

1. _____ <u>Our</u> puppy is not housetrained quite yet.

2. _____ <u>Someone</u> keeps leaving the kitchen light on.

3. _____ <u>They</u> will be attending the 9:00 performance.

4. _____ Willa wanted <u>them</u> to turn down their music.

5. _____ Carter wants to borrow <u>your</u> baseball mitt.

6. _____ Josiah dropped <u>something</u> on the bus.

7. _____ I hope that you'll be able to come to <u>my</u> graduation.

8. _____ My piano teacher asked <u>us</u> to arrive a little early.

Lesson 1.9 Action Verbs

Action verbs tell the action of the sentence. The action can be physical or mental.

> Shawn *jumped* to catch the ball (physical action)
> I *hope* your painting wins first place in the art show. (mental action)
> Please *sharpen* your pencils before the exam begins. (physical action)
> Huang *feels* lousy this morning. (mental action)
> Mr. Cooper *framed* the picture using old scraps of wood. (physical action)
> Our cat *understands* that whistling means it is time for dinner. (mental action)

Action verbs may also be in past, present, or future tense.

> A strong wind *lifted* our kites into the sky. (past)
> A strong wind *lifts* our kites into the sky. (present)
> A strong wind *will lift* our kites into the sky. (future)

Complete It

Complete each sentence with an action verb. There may be more than one correct answer, but the action verb you choose should make sense in the sentence.

1. A campfire _____ brightly enough to be seen from several miles away.

2. My mother _____ we are going to sell a lot of muffins at the bake sale today.

3. Thursday morning, Mrs. Steinfeld _____ several bags of clothing to the thrift store.

4. Some old postcards _____ silly images of people riding giant animals.

5. Karl _____ past his opponents.

6. Along the shore, ocean waves _____ over the sand and onto my feet.

7. The trees along the edge of the woods _____ .

8. Xavier _____ about the stars and planets.

9. Mongo the Magician _____ a coin from behind his ear.

10. The periodic table _____ a lot of information about chemical elements.

11. Uncle Steve _____ several custom bikes for my cousins and me.

12. I _____ soda because it has too much sugar.

Lesson 1.9 Action Verbs

Identify It

Read each sentence below. Underline action verbs that describe a physical action. Circle action verbs that describe a mental action.

1. At school yesterday, we discussed the region of Lapland.

2. I think Lapland is part of Norway, Finland, and Sweden.

3. Long ago, nomads traveled across the region in search of reindeer.

4. Lapps made their clothing from reindeer skins.

5. They preserved reindeer meat by drying or smoking it.

6. Domesticated reindeer pulled sleds and carriages.

7. I remember my teacher saying Lapps are called the Sami people today.

8. Some Sami people still herd reindeer in the 21st century.

9. Because of reindeers' thick coats, they prefer cold temperatures.

10. The subarctic climate of Lapland provides plenty of cold weather for them!

11. The zoo exhibits a small herd of reindeer in a special building.

12. I hope I get a chance to visit Lapland someday.

Try It

Write one sentence each using the five action verbs listed below.

| achieved | change | inspired | will provide | remembered |

1. _____

_____

2. _____

_____

3. _____

_____

4. _____

_____

5. _____

_____

Lesson 1.10 Subject-Verb Agreement

Subject-verb agreement means that the verb must agree in number with the subject of the sentence. If the subject is singular, use a singular verb. If the subject is plural, use a plural verb.

The <u>pinecone</u> *falls* from the tree.   The <u>pinecones</u> *fall* from the tree.

When a sentence contains a compound subject connected by the word *and*, use a plural verb.

Desiree **and** Allison *place* all the chairs beside the pool.

When a sentence contains a compound subject connected by the words *or* or *nor*, use a verb that agrees with the subject that is closer to the verb.

Neither the monkey **nor** her <u>babies</u> *eat* the leaves from that tree.
Either the girls **or** <u>Samir</u> *sweeps* the kitchen.

If the subject and the verb are separated by a word or words, be sure that the verb still agrees with the subject.

The <u>camera</u>, as well as the CDs, *is* lost.

Complete It
Complete each sentence below with the correct form of the verb in parentheses.

1. Carlos _____ coins from around the world. (collect)

2. His uncle _____ often for work. (travel)

3. Uncle Pablo and Aunt Maria _____ Carlos coins from every place they visit. (send)

4. Carlos's collection _____ up quite a bit of space in his room. (take)

5. Neither his mother nor his brothers ever _____ it. (touch)

6. Carlos _____ his collection carefully once a week. (clean)

7. The coins _____ in the sunlight from the window. (gleam)

8. Carlos's brothers _____ to buy Carlos several new coins for his birthday. (plan)

9. They _____ a great collector's shop downtown. (find)

10. Their savings _____ three unique coins for Carlos. (buy)

Lesson 1.10 Subject-Verb Agreement

Proof It

Read each sentence below. If the subject and verb agree, make a check mark on the line. If they do not agree, use proofreaders' marks to make the necessary corrections.

> _e_ – deletes a word
> ^ – inserts a word

1. _____ Aaron and his friends enjoys collecting things.

2. _____ Aaron have a collection of more than two hundred vintage stamps.

3. _____ His uncles, Clark and Will, are also philatelists, or stamp collectors.

4. _____ Neither Aaron nor his uncles collects contemporary stamps.

5. _____ Meghan looks for unusual rocks to add to her collection.

6. _____ The rocks can be common or rare, but they must be beautiful.

7. _____ Amina and Jade collects small glass figures.

8. _____ Amina, and sometimes her mother, like to look for the figures at flea markets.

9. _____ Hiromi and his older brother searches for vinyl records at yard sales.

10. _____ Shelves of records fills Hiromi's closet.

11. _____ Kerry purchases comic books online for her collection.

12. _____ Both Kerry and Owen prefers buying used comic books.

13. _____ Kerry, as well as her older brothers, has been collecting books for more than five years.

Try It

Do you enjoy collecting something? If not, what kind of collections do you think are interesting? Write several sentences about collecting. Make subjects and verbs agree.

_____

_____

_____

_____

_____

_____

_____

Lesson 1.11 Transitive and Intransitive Verbs

Transitive verbs are action verbs that are incomplete without a direct object.

> Lydia *picked* <u>some flowers</u>.

Lydia picked is not a complete sentence. The transitive verb *picked* needs a direct object (some flowers) to complete the sentence. Picked what? Some flowers.

> Malik *threw* <u>the ball</u> to his sister.

In this sentence, the transitive verb *threw* needs a direct object (the ball) to complete the sentence. Threw what? The ball.

Intransitive verbs are action verbs that do not have a direct object.

> The girls *ran* across the field.

Identify It
Read each sentence below. Underline transitive verbs once and intransitive verbs twice. For each transitive verb, circle the direct object.

1. The music pounded loudly in Finnegan's ears.

2. Mrs. Nguyen tasted the soup in the large copper pot.

3. Judge Robards sentenced the criminal to six years in prison.

4. Cody voted in the last election for the first time ever.

5. Thea told a joke at the beginning of her presentation to the class.

6. Grandpa remained on the porch late into the evening.

7. Mitzi roosted all night beside her sisters in the coop.

8. Oliver scribbled a poem on the back of his notebook.

9. Dad squealed to a stop at the red light.

10. The crumbling old letter vanished into thin air.

11. Dr. Selznick referred her patient to a specialist.

12. Have you painted a portrait of Madeline yet?

Lesson 1.11 Transitive and Intransitive Verbs

Rewrite it

The verb in each sentence below appears in boldface. On the line, write **T** if it is a transitive verb and **I** if it is intransitive. Then, rewrite the sentence using the verb in the opposite way.

Example: <u>T</u> Tia **eats** dinner at 7:00 every night.
<u>Tia eats quickly if she has basketball practice.</u>

1. _____ Joseph **walks** for miles along the beach each evening.
   _____

2. _____ The boys **played** hide-and-seek in the park all afternoon.
   _____

3. _____ Although she has just started taking lessons, Belle **draws** beautifully.
   _____

4. _____ The puppy **drank** thirstily after a long hike in the nature preserve.
   _____

5. _____ Zack's temper tantrum **spoiled** the party for his family and friends.
   _____

6. _____ Mrs. Abdul **washed** the grapes thoroughly in the sink.
   _____

7. _____ Brianna **whispered** a secret in her best friend's ear.
   _____

8. _____ Caleb **studied** after dinner each night before the examination.
   _____

Try It

Write a sentence for each of the verbs below.

Transitive verbs: sail, dig

Intransitive verbs: arrive, laugh

_____

_____

_____

_____

Lesson 1.12 Helping and Linking Verbs

Helping verbs help form the main verb in a sentence. Forms of the verbs *be*, *have*, and *do* are the most common helping verbs.

> I **have** *started* the next book in the series.
> Haley **is** *playing* the lead in the school production of "Annie."

Other helping verbs are *can, could, will, would, may, might, shall, should,* and *must.*

Linking verbs connect a subject to a noun or adjective. They do not express an action. The most common linking verbs are forms of the verb *to be*, such as *is, are, was, were, been,* and *am.*

> I *am* happy that you won the spelling bee!
> The girls *were* excited about the dance.

Other common linking verbs relate to the five senses (*smell, look, taste, feel, sound*) or a state of being (*appear, seem, become, grow, remain*).

> This sushi *tastes* fresh and delicious!
> Lauren's eyes *appear* larger behind her glasses.

Identify It

In each sentence below, circle the verb. On the line, write **LV** or **HV** to identify it as a linking verb or helping verb.

1. _____ Mary Cassatt was a famous Impressionist painter.

2. _____ Cassatt's paintings of mothers and children seem soft and gentle.

3. _____ Cassatt had learned a lot about materials and technique from her friend Edgar Degas.

4. _____ At the time, few women could pursue careers outside the home.

5. _____ Cassatt was frustrated by the narrow roles of women in society.

6. _____ Cassatt's parents would argue with their daughter.

7. _____ In Paris, Cassatt could paint with confidence.

8. _____ In Cassatt's paintings, the subjects appear very natural and at ease.

Lesson 1.12 Helping and Linking Verbs

Complete It
Read the selection below. Underline a linking verb or helping verb to complete the sentences.

People all around the world eat foods that might (seem, remain) bizarre or strange to us. The only way most Americans (could, would) eat a bug is on accident. Insects, however, (is, are) a nutritious source of protein for people in many cultures. Even in America, insects are (becoming, appearing) more popular as a sustainable choice of food. You (should, may) be surprised to learn that the practice of eating insects (have, has) a name—entomophagy. Insects (are, is) plentiful, and many are high in protein as well as vitamins and nutrients like iron, zinc, potassium, and calcium.

The witchetty grub is popular among the aborigines of Australia. When it (has been, have been) cooked, the skin (sounds, tastes) like roast chicken. When the grubs are raw, they (had, have) an almond flavor. If you are interested in trying a buggy snack, you (might, will) consider grasshoppers. Does it (appear, seem) odd to think of eating these long-legged critters? In Mexico, roasted grasshoppers are a crunchy treat. When flavored with garlic, lime, juice, and salt, they (remain, become) tasty and flavorful. Try them, and you (could, should) find that you become a fan of eating bugs. It (appears, sounds) that seeing insects on a menu may (have, be) a common occurrence in the near future.

Try It
What odd, unusual, or interesting foods have you tried? Write a short paragraph about your experience. Underline linking verbs and circle helping verbs in your paragraph.

_____

_____

_____

_____

_____

Lesson 1.13 Gerunds, Participles, and Infinitives

Gerunds, **participles**, and **infinitives** are other kinds of verbs. These verbs take the role of another part of speech in some circumstances.

A **gerund** is when a verb is used as a noun. A verb can take the form of the noun when the ending –*ing* is added.

Skiing is a great way to get outside and enjoy the winter weather.
(The subject *skiing* is a noun in the sentence.)

A **participle** is when a verb is used as an adjective. A verb can take the form of an adjective when the endings –*ing* or –*ed* are added.

The *crumbling* stones showed just how ancient the structure was.
(*crumbling* modifies *stones*)
The *stacked* boxes reached nearly to the ceiling.
(*stacked* modifies *boxes*)

An **infinitive** is when a verb is used as a noun, adjective, or adverb. A verb can take the form of a noun, adjective, or adverb when preceded by the word *to*.

To swim in the ocean is a delightful experience.
(The verb *to swim* acts as the subject, or noun, of the sentence.)
The best way *to travel* is by taking a train.
(The verb *to travel* acts as an adjective modifying *way*.)
I studied all night *to prepare* for the exam.
(The verb *to prepare* acts as an adverb modifying *studied*.)

Complete It
Complete each sentence with a word or phrase from the box. Then, place a **G** for gerund, a **P** for participle, or an **I** for infinitive on the line following the sentence to identify which was used to complete the sentence.

to drink	hanging	to capture
flapping	to lick	planting

1. _____ a photo of a hummingbird can be quite difficult. _____

2. The _____ wings of a hummingbird are almost invisible. _____

3. Hummingbirds like _____ nectar from flowers. _____

4. Hummingbirds use their long tongues _____ the nectar. _____

5. _____ the right kinds of flowers will bring hummingbirds to your yard. _____

6. You can plant the flowers in a _____ basket. _____

Lesson 1.13 Gerunds, Participles, and Infinitives

Identify It
Read the paragraph below. Underline each gerund once, underline each participle twice, and circle each infinitive.

Each kind of hummingbird has evolved to survive in a specific habitat. Chopping down trees or otherwise destroying these habitats is the greatest threat faced by hummingbirds today. Climate change is a problem as well, causing temperatures around the world to change. The result is altered migratory patterns, and the affected species fly to the wrong places. The birds struggle to find food. However, growing the right flowers in your garden will entice the hummingbirds to visit your yard and provide them with something to eat. Feeding hummingbirds is a helpful way to enjoy nature!

Try It
Make a list of six verbs. Write them on the lines below. Then, change them to gerunds, participles, and infinitives and use them in sentences. Write your new sentences on the lines provided.

_____ _____ _____

_____ _____ _____

_____

_____

_____

_____

_____

Lesson 1.14 Verb Tenses

A **present tense** verb describes an action that is happening now or happens regularly.
> The kittens *play* with a scrap of wrapping paper that fell to the floor.
> The DJ *plays* my favorite song at least once a day.

A present tense verb can also express a generalization or fact.
> The Bill of Rights *guarantees* each citizen will have certain freedoms.

A **past tense** verb describes an action that happened in the past. For many verbs, the past tense is formed by adding *-ed* to the base form of the verb.
> The maestro *conducted* the orchestra.
> The merchants at the market *dismantled* their booths before heading home.

For some verbs, the past tense is a different word.
> Emile *taught* his students how to draw using correct perspective. (past tense of *teach*)
> Construction *began* last week on the new art center downtown. (past tense of *begin*)

A **future tense** verb describes a future action. The word *will* is used before the verb.
> The train *will arrive* in Istanbul tomorrow morning.

Rewrite It
Rewrite each sentence using the indicated tense.

1. Feedback echoed through the auditorium as the crowd cheered.

Present tense: _____

2. Encyclopedias line the shelves of Dr. Noguchi's office.

Future tense: _____

3. My scanner malfunctions whenever I try to use the auto setting.

Past tense: _____

4. Sculpting tools will be offered for half their normal price.

Past tense: _____

5. A nuthatch pecked holes in the tree trunk and then flew away.

Present tense: _____

6. The photograph looks fantastic in that new frame!

Future tense: _____

Lesson 1.14 Verb Tenses

Proof It

Proofread the following paragraph. Use the proofreading marks to correct mistakes with verb tenses and irregular verbs. Insert the correctly spelled words.

> ℓ̶ – deletes a word
> ∧ – inserts a word

Yesterday, our class will visit the planetarium at the science museum downtown. After we took our seats, the museum's manager, Ms. Sanchez, speaked to us for a few minutes about the importance of studying science in school. Next, she introduces us to Dr. Kipper, the director of the planetarium. Then, the lights dim, our seats recline, and the night sky appears before our eyes. Astronomy was fascinating! We learn that the nearest star to our solar system is Proxima Centauri. It was more than 4 light years away—not exactly "near!" Dr. Kipper next will explain that Venus is the easiest planet to see. Then, he telled us more about Venus. Earth and its "sister" planet were both about the same size, have about the same amount of gravity, and are made mostly of rock. However, Venus had very little oxygen. On the next clear night, I tried to look for Venus.

Try It

Write about a recent excursion, such as a family outing to the zoo, a class field trip, or even a visit to the library. Be detailed in your description, and include both present and past tense verbs.

_____

_____

_____

_____

_____

_____

_____

_____

Lesson 1.15 Verb Tenses: Progressive

Progressive verb tenses describe ongoing, or continuing, actions.

A **present progressive** verb describes an action or condition that is ongoing in the present. A present progressive verb is made up of the present tense of the helping verb *be* and the present participle of the main verb.

> The elephant *is eating* hay.
> My dogs Friar and Tuck *are playing* in the yard.

A **past progressive** verb describes an action or condition that was ongoing at some time in the past. A past progressive verb is made up of the past form of the helping verb *be* and the present participle of the main verb.

> Bella *was practicing* ballet last night.
> The trees *were swaying* in the breeze.

Identify It
Underline the progressive verbs in each sentence. Then, write **past** or **present** on the line to identify the progressive verb tense.

1. Nadia is writing a report about Cahokia Mounds in Illinois. _____

2. Trees are growing too close to the overhead power lines. _____

3. Citizens were willing to rise up and fight their oppressors. _____

4. The microscope is magnifying a beetle's antenna. _____

5. Samuel Clemens was writing under the pseudonym Mark Twain. _____

6. The stars were shining brightly through the spacecraft's window. _____

7. Crickets are hopping ahead of me as I walk the trail. _____

8. Benny is sliding down the banister again. _____

9. Amelia was carefully dusting each little vase before gently placing it back on the shelf. _____

10. The firecrackers were exploding overhead and startling my baby brother. _____

11. Hawks are circling above the chicken coop. _____

12. A taxi is idling at the curb, ready to carry us to the airport. _____

Lesson 1.15 Verb Tenses: Progressive

Complete It
Use the past progressive forms of the verbs below to complete the paragraph.

practice	kid	approach	act	breath
wear	laugh	block	try	return
chase	kick	wait	have	save
yell	start	entertain	leap	

Brandon and his friends _____ soccer behind the athletic center, when suddenly a poodle raced across the field. The dog _____ a pink tutu, and a tall man in red suspenders _____ it. He _____, "Foofy! I _____! Come back!" The boys _____ hard because the man wore huge clown shoes and a funny wig. As he ran, the big shoes _____ up mud behind him, and the wig _____ to fall off. All at once, the man stopped. Foofy _____ the edge of the field where a fence _____ her way. She stopped too. Everyone _____ to see what would happen next. The man explained to Brandon, "We _____ at a birthday party in the park, but the kids _____ bored. I turned to Foofy and suggested we should have her jump through a ring of fire! I _____ to be funny, but Foofy _____ none of it. Next thing I knew, she _____ off the stage and headed for this field." The man _____ hard from all the running. The boys were surprised by what happened next. The man pulled a huge steak out of his pocket! In no time, Foofy _____ at full speed to the man's side. "I _____ this for after the show, but it's all yours now, Foofy." Brandon was relieved to see the man and his dog back together.

Try It
Write three verbs on the lines below. Then, use the present progressive form of each verb in a sentence.

_____   _____   _____

1. _____

2. _____

3. _____

Lesson 1.16 Verb Tenses: Perfect

Verb tenses tell when in time something happened. The **present perfect** shows that something happened in the past. The action may still be going on. The present perfect is formed with the present tense of the verb have (*have* or *has*) and a past participle.

Mae *has traveled* to Japan four times.

The **past perfect** shows that an action was completed before another action in the past. It is formed with the verb *had* and a past participle.

The lemurs *had climbed* the fence before they scaled the wall.

The **future perfect** shows that an action will be completed before a future time or a future action. It is formed with the words *will have* and a past participle.

By next week, we *will have raised* more money for the school than we did last year.

Identify It

Read each sentence below. The perfect tense verb appears in **boldface**. On the line, write **PP** if it is in past perfect, **PRP** if it is present perfect, and **FP** if it is in future perfect.

1. _____ Bianca Rodriguez and her family have **attended** the Logan County Fair every year since they moved to Indiana.

2. _____ Mrs. Betty Williams **had won** the contest for best pie six years in a row.

3. _____ Bianca **has entered** her blackberry jam in a contest.

4. _____ Her sister Rosa **had expected** to win first place for her piglets last year.

5. _____ As a judge, Mr. Rodriguez **will have tasted** more than 30 pies this year!

6. _____ Once, the Malleys' lambs **had escaped** through a hole in the fence.

7. _____ George Hankey **will have operated** the Ferris wheel for nearly two decades.

8. _____ Slim John's Ragtime Band **has played** at the south stage since the fair first began.

9. _____ Alma and Laura, Bianca's cousins, **have tried** every ride at the fair at least once.

10. _____ The rain **had poured** down for hours just before the fair started and the sun peeked out.

Lesson 1.16 Verb Tenses: Perfect

Rewrite It

Read each sentence. On the line, write the **boldface** verb in the past, present, or future perfect tense. The words in parentheses will tell you which tense to use.

1. Jess and McKenna **ask** _____ more than two hundred people to sign their petition. (present perfect)

2. Principal Jackson **lose** _____ his cell phone at the basketball game. (past perfect)

3. If he runs for class president this year, Logan **run** _____ for office three times. (future perfect)

4. Casey **earn** _____ enough money last year to buy the new bike she wanted. (past perfect)

5. Darius **miss** _____ six days of school because he had his tonsils removed. (present perfect)

6. Both Amanda and Eli **want** _____ to be yearbook editor, so they decided to share the job. (past perfect)

7. The addition to the gym **cost** _____ the school nearly half a million dollars by the time it is complete. (future perfect)

8. Keiko **play** _____ softball for two seasons before she was injured. (past perfect)

9. The kids in the astronomy club **request** _____ permission for a field trip to Lang's Planetarium. (present perfect)

10. Mr. Schneider **hope** _____ that there would be more volunteers for the science fair on Friday. (past perfect)

Try It

Write three sentences of your own about activities or hobbies you enjoy or would like to try. Write one in the past perfect, one in the present perfect, and one in the future perfect.

_____

_____

_____

_____

Review: Action Verbs, Subject-Verb Agreement, Transitive and Intransitive Verbs, Helping and Linking Verbs

Read each sentence below. Then, fill in the blank with the type of verb indicated.

1. Carter bounced the ball against the side of the brick building. action verb: _____

2. Jordan was unhappy the whole way home. helping verb: _____

3. The room suddenly seems smaller to me. linking verb: _____

4. LaTanya decided to apply for an internship this summer. action verb: _____

5. Lola has asked you at least four times. helping verb: _____

6. The glass vase shattered against the kitchen floor. action verb: _____

7. That new perfume smells terrible! linking verb: _____

8. I have not started either book yet. helping verb: _____

9. Mr. Ruben considered Brody's request for a new bike. action verb: _____

In the sentences below, circle transitive verbs and underline intransitive verbs.

1. Erik passed the ball to his brother.

2. Antonio rode his bike to the rec center after school.

3. The cat stretched lazily on the bed.

4. The girls wove bracelets for their friends.

5. The fire alarm downstairs wailed loudly.

Complete each sentence below with the correct form of the verb in parentheses.

1. Wolves _____ as a signal or a warning. (howl)

2. An adult male wolf _____ the pack. (lead)

3. Caves, burrows, and hollow logs _____ perfect dens for wolves. (make)

4. Neither wolves nor other large predators _____ liked by ranchers and farmers. (to be)

Review Chapter 1 Lessons 9–16

Review: Gerunds, Participles, Infinitives, Verb Tenses, Progressive and Perfect Tenses

Identify the underlined word using the key in the box. Write your answer on the line.

a. gerund	b. participle	c. infinitive

1. _____ Ever since she was a child, <u>swimming</u> has been Alicia's favorite activity.

2. _____ The <u>wailing</u> child drew the attention of nearly everyone at the grocery store.

3. _____ The <u>soaring</u> hawk glided along on air currents in the clear blue sky.

4. _____ If you want <u>to experience</u> a country fully, you must learn the language.

5. _____ <u>Waiting</u> has never been one of Dana's strengths.

6. _____ Derrick tried <u>to measure</u> the board as precisely as possible.

Rewrite each sentence below in the tense indicated in parentheses.

1. (present progressive) The boys hike up the side of the mountain.

   _____

2. (past progressive) Sharks circle the wounded dolphin.

   _____

3. (past progressive) Tomas practices the violin at 7:00 each night.

   _____

4. (present progressive) I print fifty copies of the election poster.

   _____

Underline the perfect tense verb in each sentence. On the line, write whether the verb is past, present, or future perfect.

1. Dr. Chandra had explained his theory to the class last week. _____

2. Meghan has eaten escargots, or snails, four times. _____

3. Eli will have visited each of the fifty states at least once by the year 2018.

   _____

4. We had called everyone on the list of names. _____

5. The Esgrows have visited the Vietnam Veterans' Memorial every summer.

   _____

Lesson 1.17 Adjectives and Predicate Adjectives

An **adjective** is a word that describes a noun or pronoun. It offers more information about the word it modifies. Adjectives often come before the noun or pronoun they describe. They answer the question *What kind? How many?* or *Which one?*

    The *heavy* rain beat down upon the *drooping* sunflowers.

    Sofia's *shiny black* shoes reflected the *bright* lights of the *sparkling* chandelier.

Proper adjectives are capitalized.

    Lola ordered *French* fries with her sandwich.

    The *Russian* president appeared in several news articles about the event.

A **predicate adjective** follows a linking verb (a form of the verb *to be, smell, look, taste, feel, sound, appear, seem, become, grow,* or *remain*). A predicate adjective modifies the subject of the sentence.

    The apples <u>smelled</u> *sweet* as Ivana dropped them into her basket.

In this example, *sweet* is a predicate adjective, following the linking verb *smelled*. It modifies *apples,* the subject of the sentence.

Identify It

Underline each common or proper adjective you find. Circle the predicate adjectives.

1. Easter eggs usually come in pretty pastel colors.

2. Picture pink, yellow, and purple eggs nestled into baskets filled with sweet treats and faux grass.

3. Ukrainian eggs, however, are different.

4. *Pysanky* are gorgeous eggs decorated with folk designs.

5. According to tradition, the eggs are dyed with dyes made from colorful flowers, plants, and berries.

6. Heated beeswax is applied to the egg, and then a layer of color is added.

7. In between each layer of color, more beautiful, intricate designs are added.

8. The egg appears lumpy with the beeswax markings.

9. Finally, the entire egg is heated so that the warm wax can be removed.

10. A *pysanka* is special—a gift that has been created with care and time.

Lesson 1.17 Adjectives and Predicate Adjectives

Complete It
Each sentence below is missing at least one adjective. Fill in each blank with an adjective. When you are done, circle all the predicate adjectives you used. There is more than one correct answer for each item.

1. The _____ sunset over the lake was _____.

2. The _____ smell of rotten eggs quickly filled the house.

3. Ian opened the _____ book, and the smell of _____ paper and ink drifted into the room.

4. Tess sat at the _____ desk and rested her feet on the _____ back of her _____ dog.

5. Ramona felt _____ as she watched her _____ son board the _____ school bus.

6. Anders collapsed onto the _____ bed, crying _____ tears into his pillow.

7. The music sounded _____, like opening the window on _____ day.

8. Tanisha chased the ball down the field, brushing her _____ hair from her eyes.

9. The baby grew _____ as the _____ sky filled with _____ stars.

10. My sister and I carved the _____ pumpkin, adding a _____ mouth filled with _____ teeth.

Try It
Describe the most beautiful or unusual place you've ever visited.
Use at least eight adjectives in your description.

_____

_____

_____

_____

_____

_____

_____

_____

Lesson 1.18 Comparative and Superlative Adjectives

Comparative adjectives compare two nouns, and **superlative adjectives** compare three or more nouns.

> neat, neater, neatest   ugly, uglier, ugliest   wise, wiser, wisest

For adjectives that end in *y*, change *y* to *i* before adding the suffixes *–er* or *–est*.

> silly, sillier, silliest   sunny, sunnier, sunniest

Comparing two nouns:

> The store on this side of town is *newer* than the store across town.
> The pasta salad looks like a *tastier* dish than the potato salad.

Comparing three or more nouns:

> The end of school is the *craziest* time of year.
> I want to take the *prettiest* way home.

Comparative and superlative adjectives can also be formed by adding the words *more* (comparative) and *most* (superlative) before the adjective. Use *more* and *most* with longer adjectives that have two or more syllables.

> That is the *most expensive* pair of sneakers I've ever seen!
> Connor becomes *more curious* about that package every day.

Match It

Draw a line to match the sentence blanks in Column A with the adjectives in Column B.

Column A	**Column B**
1. Of the three assignments, this one is the _____.	busier
2. The weather today is supposed to be _____ than it was yesterday.	stranger
3. I'll take the _____ of the two classes so I'll finish sooner.	earlier
4. Because of the deadlines, I'm _____ this week than next.	easiest
5. Which of the two movies did you think was _____?	gentler
6. I love spicy foods. I want to order the _____ of the two dishes.	spicier
7. Our new dog is much _____ than the wild puppy we used to have.	milder
8. Out of all the bouquets we saw, I think the one with the tulips is the _____.	creamiest
9. Use my recipe, and you will have the _____ guacamole you've ever tasted.	loveliest

Lesson 1.18 Comparative and Superlative Adjectives

Complete It
Write the correct form of the adjective in parentheses to complete each sentence below.

1. I am _____ in these jeans than in any of my other pants. (comparative of *comfortable*)

2. Aunt Wendy became _____ after her two cats passed away. (comparative of *lonely*)

3. The weather on Saturday was the _____ we've had in weeks. (superlative of *lovely*)

4. Professor Halliday's lecture about black holes was the _____ lecture I've heard this year! (superlative of *interesting*)

5. The water in this tide pool is much _____ than it is where you are standing. (comparative of *shallow*)

6. Cecile's drawing of the human skeletal system is the _____ I've ever seen. (superlative of *precise*)

7. Bill has got a wonderful secret recipe for the _____ fried chicken you've ever had. (superlative of *crispy*)

8. Detective Tang became _____ each time she saw Roland enter the building. (comparative of *suspicious*)

9. Are the gems that Ramon found _____ than the ones his brother found? (comparative of *rare*)

10. Jess is _____ about animals since she began working at a veterinary practice. (comparative of *compassionate*)

Try It
Write a sentence following the instruction for each item below.

1. Use the comparative of *frustrating*. _____

2. Use the superlative of *narrow*. _____

3. Use the comparative of *simple*. _____

4. Use the superlative of *trustworthy*. _____

Lesson 1.19 Adverbs and Intensifiers

Adverbs modify, or describe, verbs. An adverb tells how, when, or where an action occurs.

> The audience cheered *wildly*. (tells *how* the audience cheered)
> We arrived at the restaurant *late*. (tells *when* we arrived)
> Max tossed the ball *over* the basket. (tells *where* Max tossed the ball)

Adverbs can also modify adjectives or other adverbs.

> The field of snow was *blindingly* white. (*blindingly* modifies the adjective *white*)
> Mr. Langstrom called our house *unusually* early this morning. (*unusually* modifies the adverb *early*)

Many, but not all, adverbs are formed by adding *–ly* to adjectives.

Intensifiers are adverbs that add emphasis or intensity to adjectives or other adverbs. The following are common intensifiers.

almost	extremely	just	nearly	practically	quite	rather
really	so	somewhat	such	too	very	

> Kwan is *too* young to join the varsity swim team.
> The seamstress *quite* carelessly tore a hole in the pants.

Identify It

Circle the adverb or intensifier in each sentence. Underline the word that is being modified.

1. The drivers raced extremely quickly around the track's curves.

2. The blackberries ripened to a deep purple color.

3. Each contestant excitedly approached the prize table.

4. The Big Dipper is really easy to spot on a clear night.

5. Lance accidentally knocked his funny bone against the chair.

6. Dr. Greta aimed the laser up toward the moon.

7. Snow fell soundlessly from the sky.

8. Plants grow so slowly, you cannot see them move.

Lesson 1.19 Adverbs and Intensifiers

Complete It

Fill in each blank with an adverb or intensifier. Use the words shown in the box, either to fill in blanks or for ideas. Be sure the words make sense where you place them in the sentences.

too	very	practically	politely	helpfully	truly
lately	quite	initially	happily	mostly	freshly
carefully	originally	outside	desperately	quickly	generously
grumpily	only	barely	much	so	
icily	obviously	especially	profusely	such	
helpfully	reluctantly	gently	eagerly	loudly	

_____ early Wednesday morning, Natasha's alarm rang _____. The noise startled her from a _____ dreamy sleep. She was _____ annoyed, but then she _____ recalled why she had to arise _____ early. Today, Natasha would begin _____ volunteering at the local food pantry. The pantry _____ provided meals for those in need. The breakfast shift was _____ important. A child could get a _____ made breakfast before heading to school. Natasha _____ dressed and rushed _____ down the stairs. The sun _____ peaked above the horizon, so the sky was _____ still dark. Natasha had _____ planned to bike to the pantry, because it was not _____ far from her home. Then, she looked _____ at the thermometer hanging _____ near the window. The temperature was _____ cold at just 22°! Natasha _____ shivered at the thought of riding in_____ freezing weather. Instead, she trudged _____ back up the stairs and tapped _____ at her _____ older brother's door. She heard Walt _____ ask, "What?" But when she _____ explained why she _____ needed a ride, he jumped _____ out of bed. He was _____ impressed with Natasha and _____ willing to help. It took _____ a few minutes to drive to the pantry. Natasha thanked her brother _____ before heading into the building, a huge grin _____ adorning her face.

Try It

Write a short descriptive paragraph about traveling through a desert. Include at least four adverbs in your description.

_____

_____

_____

Lesson 1.20 Comparative and Superlative Adverbs

Like comparative adjectives, **comparative adverbs** compare two actions.
> Our tennis team played *more skillfully* than their team.
> Lana went to bed *later* than Maurice.

Superlative adverbs compare three or more actions.
> The Larkins' home is the *most beautifully* decorated house on the block.
> The Number 12 bus arrived *soonest*.

Short adverbs are formed using *–er* for comparatives and *–est* for superlatives. Long adverbs use the words *more* or *most*, or for negative comparisons, use *less* or *least*.
> The sun rose *earlier* this morning than it did yesterday.
> The sun rises *earliest* on the morning of the summer solstice.
> Sven yelled *more enthusiastically* than his dad did when the Red Sox won.
> Mr. Kline acted *least enthusiastically* about the win.

Some comparative and superlative adverbs do not follow these patterns. The following are examples of irregular comparative and superlative adverbs.
> well, better, best   badly, worse, worst

Rewrite It
Rewrite each sentence below using a comparative or superlative adverb.
1. Claude stared seriously at the unfinished painting.

comparative: _____

2. The cardinal flew quietly out of its nest.

superlative: _____

3. The team of scientists arrives soon.

comparative: _____

4. Frank's Fish was reviewed favorably in our local paper.

comparative: _____

5. I am eagerly awaiting the visit with my Uncle Lenny.

superlative: _____

6. Hanna looked obviously annoyed about the e-mail.

comparative: _____

7. Ms. Rain smiled happily when the phone rang.

superlative: _____

Lesson 1.20 Comparative and Superlative Adverbs

Proof It

Proofread the following sentences. Use the proofreading marks to correct mistakes with comparative and superlative adverbs.

1. The monkeys reacted curiosousliest to the bananas presented on trays.

2. I felt more bad about missing my brother's swim meet.

e	– deletes a word
^	– inserts a word

3. Mae arranged her clothes least sloppily than Rachel did.

4. Those sheep seem to eat greedilier than the pigs.

5. The moon's gravity pulls less stronger than Earth's gravity does.

6. Lucy finished her lunch more early than the other students.

7. The builders worked feverishlier when they learned they could earn a bonus.

8. I study most well when I have some quiet music playing.

9. The van was parked more close to the curb.

10. The hands on the clock move more slowest if you feel bored.

11. Mr. Hanson awarded the students who behaved properliest during the performance.

12. Darnell's trip to the dentist went smoothlier than he had expected.

13. Oscar traveled most comfortable when sitting in an aisle seat.

14. At business school, Beth spoke more professionaler than she did at home.

15. Of all Stella's animals, the dogs wait less patiently.

Try It

Choose six adverbs from the box. For three of them, write three sentences using the comparative form. For the other three, write three sentences using the superlative form.

quickly	soon	delicately	graciously	sleepily
happily	affectionately	eagerly	critically	carelessly
sluggishly	often	far	closely	lovingly

1. _____

2. _____

3. _____

4. _____

5. _____

6. _____

Lesson 1.21 Adjectives and Adverbs

Some adjectives and adverbs are easy to confuse with one another. Use a predicate adjective after a linking verb (forms of the verb *to be* and verbs like *seem, taste, grow,* and *become*). Use an adverb to describe an action verb.

The music <u>sounded</u> *joyful* as it streamed through the open windows.

Zora <u>played</u> *joyfully*, as though a large audience was listening.

In first example, the adjective *joyful* follows the linking verb *sounded* and modifies the subject *music*. In the second example, the adverb *joyfully* modifies the action verb *played*.

The words *good, well, bad,* and *badly* are often used incorrectly. *Good* and *bad* are adjectives, and *well* and *badly* are adverbs.

Your homemade yogurt <u>tastes</u> *good*.

The milk you bought last week <u>is</u> *bad*.

Daisy <u>behaved</u> *badly* at the groomer's on Friday.

Bubbles and Ringo <u>ate</u> *well* today, even though they were sick last night.

Match It

Match each sentence to the adjective or adverb that completes it. On the line, write the letter of your choice.

1. _____ The noise was _____ and startled the grackles in the oak tree.
    a. sudden
    b. suddenly

2. _____ The chipmunk darted _____ across the yard.

3. _____ Toshi felt _____ as he waited in line at the post office.
    a. impatiently
    b. impatient

4. _____ Samuel waited _____ while his sister put on her shoes.

5. _____ Felix watched _____ as his team scored another goal.
    a. eagerly
    b. eager

6. _____ The children grew _____ as the first snowflake started to fall.

7. _____ Kara performed _____ after a long, sleepless night.
    a. bad
    b. badly

8. _____ Joshua felt _____ that he had missed Kara's performance.

9. _____ Ms. Hennessy appeared _____, but I knew she was nervous.
    a. calm
    b. calmly

10. _____ Although the weather was rough, the pilot flew _____.

Lesson 1.21 Adjectives and Adverbs

Identify It
Read each item below. On the line, write **Adj.** or **Adv.** to identify each **boldface** word as an adjective or adverb. If the word is an adjective, underline the linking verb it follows. If the word is an adverb, circle the action verb it follows.

1. _____ The pink peony that Elena chose smelled **fragrant**.

2. _____ Mittens meowed **cheerfully** at Mia's door at six o'clock in the morning.

3. _____ It rained all night, but the next morning, the sun shone **brightly**.

4. _____ The rickety wooden bridge appeared **unsafe**, but Justin decided to take his chances.

5. _____ Although we were in a rural area, our cell phone reception was **good**.

6. _____ Quinn was no expert, but the cheese tasted **rancid**.

7. _____ Aunt Ella looked **elegant** in the cherry red ball gown.

8. _____ Grandma Sheryl claims that she never sleeps **well** in a hotel room.

9. _____ The door closed **completely**, even before Mickey had finished speaking.

10. _____ O'Connor made the basket, and the crowd cheered **wildly**.

11. _____ The auditorium grew **quiet** as Mr. Hague took the stage.

12. _____ After spending most of the day in the car, the boys acted **badly** at dinner.

Try It
Write two sentences containing adverbs and two containing adjectives.

1. _____

_____

2. _____

_____

3. _____

_____

4. _____

_____

Lesson 1.22 Prepositions and Prepositional Phrases

Prepositions are words that show the relationship between a noun or pronoun and another word in the sentence.

The truck ran *off* the road.   The garbage can is *beside* the fence.

Some common prepositions are *above, across, after, along, around, at, away, because, before, behind, below, beneath, beside, between, by, down, during, except, for, from, in, into, near, off, on, outside, over, to, toward, under, until, up, with, within,* and *without*.

Prepositional phrases include the prepositions and the objects (nouns or pronouns) that follow the prepositions. A prepositional phrase includes the preposition, the object of the preposition, and the modifiers of the object. Prepositional phrases tell *when* or *where* something is happening.

The calico cat hid *under the white bookshelf.* (Where? Under the white bookshelf)
Anson woke up *before his brother.* (When? Before his brother)

Complete It
Each sentence below is missing a preposition. Complete the sentences with prepositions from the box. There may be than one correct answer for each item.

for	from	to	with	during
by	around	off	beneath	in

1. An iceberg is a large piece of ice that floats _____ open water.

2. The word *iceberg* comes _____ a Dutch word that means "ice mountain."

3. Most of an iceberg lies _____ the water; only about one-tenth is above the water.

4. A dome iceberg is an iceberg _____ a rounded top.

5. Today, icebergs are monitored _____ the U.S. National Ice Center.

6. Most icebergs are formed _____ the spring and summer.

7. An iceberg was responsible _____ the sinking of the *Titanic.*

8. Even today, icebergs can cause great damage _____ a ship.

9. Most of the world's icebergs are found _____ Antarctica and Greenland.

10. When a chunk of ice calves, it breaks _____ a glacier and an iceberg is formed.

Lesson 1.22 Prepositions and Prepositional Phrases

Identify It

Underline each prepositional phrase in the sentences below. Circle each preposition. The number in parentheses will tell you how many prepositions each sentence contains.

1. The *Titanic* was a luxury passenger ship that sailed from Southampton, England. (1)

2. The awesome ship collided with an iceberg. (1)

3. The iceberg came from a glacier in Greenland. (2)

4. The *Titanic* sank on its maiden voyage. (1)

5. The remains of the great boat lie more than 12,000 feet beneath the ocean's surface. (2)

6. The *Titanic* used 825 tons of coal every day. (1)

7. It took 74 years to locate the wreck of the Titanic. (1)

8. When the *Titanic* set sail, she was the largest human-made moving object on Earth. (1)

9. During its voyage, the *Titanic* did not hold any lifeboat drills for the passengers. (2)

10. After the wreck, hundreds of stories were written about the ill-fated voyage. (3)

Try It

Write a short paragraph about a momentous news event that has occurred during your lifetime. Underline each preposition you use.

_____

_____

_____

_____

_____

_____

_____

Lesson 1.23 Conjunctions and Interjections

Conjunctions connect individual words or groups of words in sentences.

Coordinate conjunctions connect words, phrases, or independent clauses that are equal or of the same type. Coordinate conjunctions are *and, but, or, nor, for,* and *yet.*
>The satin dress felt smooth *and* silky beneath Anna's fingers.

Correlative conjunctions come in pairs and are used together. *Both/and, either/or,* and *neither/nor* are examples of correlative conjunctions.
>*Neither* Michael *nor* Aiden can join us tonight.

Subordinate conjunctions connect dependent clauses to independent clauses in order to complete the meaning. *After, although, as long as, since, unless, whether,* and *while* are examples of subordinate conjunctions.
>*Whether* it snows or not, we will go to the play tomorrow.

An **interjection** is a word or phrase used to express surprise or strong emotion. Common interjections include:

ah	alas	aw	awesome	eeek	hey	hi
hurray	oh	oh, no	oops	ouch	phew	wow

An exclamation mark or a comma is used after an interjection to separate it from the rest of the sentence.
>*Oops!* I dropped the glass!   *Oh,* I'm sorry to hear that!

Complete It
Complete each of the following sentences with an interjection of your choosing.

  1. _____! I burned my hand on the stove!

  2. _____, that is probably the last chance we'll have to talk with Professor Snoddkins.

  3. _____! That was a close call!

  4. _____, what a beautiful bouquet of tulips!

  5. _____! I'm so happy all your hard work paid off!

  6. _____, that's exactly what I thought would happen!

Lesson 1.23 Conjunctions and Interjections

Identify It

Read the phrases in the box. Write them beside the appropriate headings.

the ladybugs or the aphids	**unless you can find the book**
the green and yellow shirts	**both the wrench and the hammer**
since Pablo left for school after the storm	**likes shrimp but hates fish**
neither the mangoes nor the kiwis	**either on Monday or on Wednesday**

Coordinate Conj._____

_____

Correlative Conj.   _____

_____

Subordinate Conj.   _____

_____

Try It

For each number below, write a sentence that includes the items in parentheses.

1. (a correlative conjunction)_____

_____

2. (a subordinate conjunction) _____

_____

3. (an interjection) _____

_____

4. (a subordinate conjunction and a coordinate conjunction) _____

_____

5. (an interjection and a correlative conjunction) _____

_____

6. (two coordinate conjunctions) _____

_____

7. (a correlative conjunction)_____

_____

Review Chapter I Lessons 17–23

Review: Adjectives and Predicate Adjectives, Comparative and Superlative Adjectives, Adverbs and Intensifiers, Comparative and Superlative Adverbs

Identify the adjective in each sentence. If it is a predicate adjective, underline it. Circle the other adjectives. On the line, write **C** if the adjective is comparative, write **S** if the adjective is superlative, and leave the line blank if the adjective is neither comparative nor superlative.

I. _____ The tallest mountain in the world, measured from its base, is Mauna Koa.

2. _____ You may not recognize the name, but Mauna Koa is famous.

3. _____ This mountain is the beautiful island of Hawaii.

4. _____ Mt. Everest, however, is higher above Earth's surface.

5. _____ Mt. Everest towers over the forbidding landscape of Tibet.

6. _____ Tenzing Norgay and Edmund Hillary completed the first ascent in 1953.

7. _____ The ascent may be treacherous, but thousands have climbed to Everest's peak since then.

8. _____ Considering the mountain's remoteness, the area is messier than you might imagine.

9. _____ Abandoned gear lies scattered along the trail to the top.

10. _____ Artists from Nepal came up with a creative idea.

11. _____ They turned the worthless junk into art!

12. _____ Art galleries were enthusiastic about the idea.

As indicated, rewrite each sentence to change the adverb to a comparative or superlative adverb. If the sentence contains an intensifier, circle the intensifier.

I. Raj typed quickly because he was almost out of time.

Comparative: _____

2. Mr. Lincoln was extremely tired this evening, so he trudged sleepily up the stairs.

Comparative: _____

3. The kayak raced speedily through the rapids.

Superlative: _____

4. My friend plays soccer well when he has had a big breakfast.

Superlative: _____

Review Chapter 1 Lessons 17–23

Review: Adjectives and Adverbs, Prepositions and Prepositional Phrases, Conjunctions and Interjections

Circle the correct adjective or adverb to complete each sentence.

1. Mr. Louis feels (bad, badly) about missing the performance.

2. The entire class felt (cheerfully, cheerful) after a visit from Officer Bunkley.

3. I did (good, well) on my algebra test.

4. Nan waited (impatiently, impatient) for the receptionist to call her name.

5. Lying in bed, Brie could hear (quiet, quietly) raindrops tapping the window.

Identify the boldface word in each sentence. On the line, write **P** if it is a preposition, **C** if it is a conjunction, or **I** if it is an interjection. For sentences that contain a preposition, also underline the prepositional phrase.

1. _____ **Wow**, you really know how to juggle, don't you?

2. _____ The robin landed **on** the birdfeeder.

3. _____ **Whenever** Trent mows the lawn, he also uses the weed whacker.

4. _____ We will be studying the Civil War **until** the semester ends.

5. _____ The dog barks all night, **yet** he never sleeps during the day.

6. _____ **Oops**, I didn't mean to close that window yet.

7. _____ Rudy **and** his sister will be visiting Atlanta next week.

8. _____ The Ingalls bought their horses **from** a breeder in Kentucky.

9. _____ Wind this string **around** the stake at the end of the yard.

10. _____ Please give this note to Mr. Rickert **while** you are at his office.

Write a sentence that contains two prepositional phrases:_____

_____

Write a sentence that contains a coordinate conjunction: _____

_____

Write a sentence that contains a correlative conjunction: _____

_____

Write a sentence that contains a subordinate conjunction:_____

_____

Lesson 1.24 Sentence Types

A **declarative sentence** makes a statement about a place, person, thing, or idea, and it ends with a period.

> Cirrus clouds look like wispy smears of white in the blue sky.

An **interrogative sentence** asks a question and ends with a question mark.

> Why do airplanes sometimes leave long, white trails through the sky?

An **exclamatory sentence** shows urgency, strong surprise, or emotion, and ends with an exclamation mark.

> That sunset is so beautiful!

An **imperative sentence** demands that an action be performed. The subject of an imperative sentence is usually not expressed, but the subject is normally understood as *you*. Imperative sentences can be punctuated with a period or an exclamation mark.

> Hand me the binoculars, please.
> Look at that funnel cloud!

Rewrite It

Rewrite each sentence so it provides an example of the indicated sentence type.

1. Fog is a stratus cloud that has formed at ground level.

Interrogative: _____

2. Cumulonimbus clouds can reach heights of 60,000 feet.

Exclamatory: _____

3. Can you please grab my book about clouds?

Imperative: _____

4. What does *nimbus* mean when it appears at the end of a cloud name?

Imperative: _____

5. Is *nimbus* the Latin word for "shower"?

Declarative: _____

6. A "mackerel sky" is known scientifically as cirrocumulus clouds.

Interrogative:_____

Lesson 1.24 Sentence Types

Identify It
Read the passage below. Use the line following each sentence to identify the sentence type. Write **D** for declarative, **IN** for interrogative, **E** for exclamatory, and **IM** for imperative.

Turn your eyes to the sky and describe what's there. _____ Is it all blue? _____ Then, your job will be fairly easy. _____ How do you describe the different kinds of clouds, though? _____ If you're a poet, you're free to use metaphors and other figurative language. _____ If you're a scientist, you need to be more precise. _____ In the early 1800s, Englishman Luke Howard devised a system for describing clouds based on their appearances. _____ He classified clouds into three categories: cirrus, stratus, and cumulus. _____ Have you ever seen delicate, wispy clouds that look like they were painted onto the sky by a brush? _____ Those are cirrus clouds, and they form more than 20,000 feet above the ground. _____ That's way up there! _____

Stratus clouds are found lower, at an altitude of between 6,000 and 20,000 feet. _____ Try to guess how stratus clouds look. _____ If I gave you a hint, would it help? _____ Drizzle or light snow often falls from stratus clouds. _____ Did you guess that stratus clouds appear as an overcast sky? _____ Then, you're right! _____ When stratus clouds are overhead, it looks like a smooth ceiling of white or gray has moved across the sky. _____

So what about big, puffy white clouds drifting through the sky on a summer day? _____ Those are cumulus clouds. _____ They don't usually bring rain, but on a steamy day a cumulus cloud can grow bigger and bigger until it's a cumulonimbus cloud. _____ Take cover! _____ A cumulonimbus cloud is also known as a thunderhead, most likely bringing thunder, lightning, and heavy rain as it rolls over the land. _____

Try It
On the lines below, write one example each of the four sentence types.

Declarative:_____

Interrogative:_____

Exclamatory: _____

Imperative:_____

Lesson 1.25 Simple and Compound Sentences

An **independent clause** presents a complete thought and can stand alone as a sentence.

Simple sentences are sentences with one independent clause. Simple sentences can have one or more subjects and one or more predicates.

The players huddled in the middle of the field. (one subject, one predicate)
The players and *the coaches* huddled in the middle of the field. (two subjects, one predicate)
The players and the coaches *huddled in the middle* of the field and *discussed the next play*. (two subjects, two predicates)

Compound sentences are sentences with two or more simple sentences, or independent clauses. A compound sentence can be two sentences joined with a comma and a coordinate conjunction. The most common coordinating conjunctions are *and, but, or, yet*, and *so. For* and *nor* can also act as coordinating conjunctions.

Eli handed the ball to Terrell, but Terrell fumbled it.
A compound sentence can also be two simple sentences joined by a semicolon.

Eli handed the ball to Terrell; Terrell fumbled it.

Match It
Match a simple sentence from Column A with a simple sentence from Column B to create a compound sentence. Write each compound sentence on the lines below, and remember to add either a coordinate conjunction or punctuation.

Column A

1. The first Super Bowl was played in January 1967.

2. It featured the best team of the AFL against the best team of the NFL.

3. The Kansas City Chiefs were the AFL champions.

4. The first half of the game was competitive.

5. Packers' Quarterback Bart Starr scored two touchdowns and threw for 250 yards.

Column B

1. The Green Bay Packers were the NFL champions.

2. Bart Starr was named Most Valuable Player.

3. Some people called it the Supergame.

4. The game would determine the best football team in America.

5. The second half of the game was determined by the Packers.

1. _____

2. _____

3. _____

4. _____

5. _____

Lesson 1.25 Simple and Compound Sentences

Identify It
Read each sentence and determine whether it is a simple or compound sentence. On the line at the beginning of the sentence, write **S** for simple or **C** for compound. On the two lines following the sentence, identify the total number of subjects and predicates in each sentence.

1. _____ The referee blew her whistle, and both teams rushed onto the field.
    S: _____ **P:** _____

2. _____ The Western Wildcats and the Northside Knights had played each other earlier in the season, but tonight's game was the regional championship.
    S: _____ **P:** _____

3. _____ Eli took the snap and hurled the ball downfield. **S:** _____ **P:** _____

4. _____ Brandon leaped for the ball, but Jamal was there first. **S:** _____ **P:** _____

5. _____ The crowd roared, jumped to its feet, and then groaned; Jamal could not hold on to the ball, and he dropped it. **S:** _____ **P:** _____

6. _____ The next play was less exciting, for Eli handed off the ball for no gain.
    S: _____ **P:** _____

7. _____ Eli's father yelled and caught the attention of a vendor; she sold him three hot dogs. **S:** _____ **P:** _____

8. _____ Eli had run straight up the middle and scored a touchdown, but his father was buying hot dogs and missed it. **S:** _____ **P:** _____

9. _____ The team grabbed Eli and hoisted him onto their shoulders.
    S: _____ **P:** _____

10. _____ They carried him back to the sidelines and set him down by the coach.
    S: _____ **P:** _____

11. _____ The coach and several other players gave Eli high-fives. **S:** _____ **P:** _____

12. _____ Eli's father ate the hot dogs, but he didn't buy anything else for the rest of the game. **S:** _____ **P:** _____

Try It
Write a paragraph about a sporting event you attended or took part in. Include a variety of simple and compound sentences in your description.

_____

_____

_____

_____

_____

Lesson 1.26 Complex Sentences

A **dependent clause** does not present a complete thought and cannot stand alone as sentence.

Complex sentences have one independent clause and one or more dependent clauses. The independent and dependent clauses are connected with a subordinate conjunction or a relative pronoun. The dependent clause can be anywhere in the sentence.

Complex sentence (connected with subordinate conjunction):

    The metric system is easy to use *because* the units are based on multiples of 10.

Complex sentence (connected with a relative pronoun):

    I just finished a biography of Muhammad Ali, *who* everybody knows is the greatest boxer of all time.

The dependent clause can either be the first or second part of the sentence.

    Before you can water the garden, you need to turn on the spigot at the house.

    You need to turn on the spigot at the house *before* you can water the garden.

Complete It

For each unfinished complex sentence, choose a subordinate conjunction from the list and use it to write the missing part. Use a different word from the list for each sentence.

after	if	unless	where
although	once	until	wherever
because	since	when	whether
before	though	whenever	while

1. _____, Jack will join us for the celebration.

2. The snow fell continuously for nearly three hours _____.

3. Dr. Murray emptied the cupboards above the sink _____.

4. _____, the lumberjacks spent the weekend in town.

5. Most of William's friends ride home on Bus #19 _____.

6. _____, the garbage truck hauls its load to the dump.

7. _____, cupcakes decorated as ladybugs will be a hit!

8. You can't join the Rocky Ridge Nature Club _____.

9. Hazel's favorite rollercoaster zips downhill at more than 100 m.p.h.

_____.

10. _____, storm clouds moved quickly across the horizon and blocked the setting sun.

Lesson 1.26 Complex Sentences

For each sentence, circle the subordinate conjunction and underline the dependent clause.

1. Although its official name is *Cloud Gate*, most Chicagoans refer to Anish Kapoor's famous sculpture as "The Bean."

2. The beautiful mirrored surface is hard to describe unless you've seen it in person.

3. Kapoor was born in India in 1954 and lived there until he moved to Britain in the early 1970s.

4. He was awarded the Turner Prize in 2002, which is a very prestigious honor given annually to the best British artist under 50 years old.

5. Whenever most people visit Chicago, a trip to see "The Bean" is on their list of things to do.

6. Visitors can walk right under the sculpture because the arched shape underneath it is 12 feet high.

7. Be sure to bring a camera when you visit.

8. The curved surfaces create distorted reflections that make great photographs.

9. After you visit "The Bean," you can find other interesting activities nearby.

10. Since the sculpture is located in Millennium Park, you'll have just a short walk to ice-skating, gardens, and another fun public artwork, *Crown Fountain*.

11. Although *Crown Fountain* is a piece of art, it's also a place to play.

12. Water cascades down the 50-foot tall glass walls of the fountain while LED lights behind the glass project videos.

13. Unless it's a really cold day, visitors play in the water falling down the wall and collecting in a pool at the base.

14. I recommend a visit to Chicago's Millennium Park if you get the chance.

15. Whether you like dancing in fountains, ice-skating, or seeing great public art, you're sure to enjoy it.

Try It

Write five complex sentences on the lines below. Use subordinate conjunctions in four of the sentences and a relative pronoun in the fifth sentence.

1. _____

2. _____

3. _____

4. _____

5. _____

Lesson 1.27 Adjective and Adverb Clauses

An **adjective clause** is a dependent clause that modifies a noun or pronoun. An adjective clause usually follows the word it modifies. The clause begins with a relative pronoun, such as *that, which, who, whom, whose,* or *whoever.*

Mira's sister, *who you saw at a dance recital,* sprained her ankle.
Cockroaches carry bacteria *that may cause food poisoning.*

An **adverb clause** is a dependent clause that modifies a verb, an adjective, or an adverb. An adverb clause answers the question *How? When? Where? Why?* or *Under what condition?* The first word of an adverb clause is a subordinate conjunction, such as *although, until, once, however, unless, if,* or *while.*

Until Grandpa retires, he will continue to get up at 5:30 A.M.
I'll walk to school tomorrow *if it isn't raining.*

Complete It
Each boldface adjective clause below is missing a relative pronoun. Each boldface adverb clause is missing a subordinate conjunction. Choose a relative pronoun or subordinate conjunction from the box and write it on the line to complete the sentence.

Relative Pronouns

whom	which	that	whoever	who

Subordinate Conjunctions

when	unless	if	whenever	while

1. The moonflower, _____ **is a member of the morning glory family,** blooms in the evening.

2. You will miss Justin's speech _____ **you don't hurry.**

3. The girl _____ **won the spelling bee** rides my bus.

4. Emil volunteers at the food bank _____ **he has the time.**

5. It is unusual for rain to fall _____ **the sun is out.**

6. Sadie is a friend _____ **you've met** several times.

7. Roasted chickpeas are a crunchy treat _____ **you would like.**

8. _____ **you are an expert in edible plants,** it is best not to eat things that grow in the wild.

9. _____ **we go to the market,** Mom buys fresh goat cheese.

10. The person with muddy feet, _____ **that may be,** needs to clean the floors.

Lesson 1.27 Adjective and Adverb Clauses

Identify It
Read the sentences below. Circle the adjective clauses, and underline the adverb clauses.

1. African wild dogs, which live south of Africa's Sahara Desert, are similar to wolves.

2. Although they are called "dogs," these animals are definitely wild, not domesticated.

3. Since African wild dogs have unique patterns, it is easy to distinguish them from one another.

4. Dr. McNutt, who studies African wild dogs, hopes to educate people about these rare and unusual animals.

5. Whereas there are millions of domestic dogs, only about 6,000 wild African dogs remain.

6. Something must be done before the numbers of wild dogs sinks even lower.

7. Because they are fast runners, wild dogs can hunt animals like gazelles, antelope, and birds.

8. Wild dogs that attack cows and sheep on ranches may be shot.

9. Ranch owners, whose livelihood depends on their livestock, have little patience for wild dogs.

10. The sounds wild dogs make are meaningless unless you know what to listen for.

Try It
Why are wild animals worth saving? Write several sentences about your views. Circle the adjective clauses and underline the adverb clauses in your answer.

_____

_____

_____

_____

Review Chapter 1 Lessons 24–27

Review: Sentence Types, Simple and Compound Sentences

Read the sentences below. Use the line following each sentence to identify the sentence type. Write **D** for declarative, **IN** for interrogative, **E** for exclamatory, and **IM** for imperative.

1. Are you familiar with the artwork of pop artist Andy Warhol? _____

2. If you haven't seen it before, you might be surprised! _____

3. Andy's mother taught him to draw when he was eight years old and was ill with a liver disease. _____

4. In 1961, Andy had a unique idea about using mass-produced commercial products in his art. _____

5. Would you consider an image of a soup can, repeated over and over in different colors, to be art? _____

6. Andy also used images of celebrities, such as Marilyn Monroe and Che Guevara, in his artwork. _____

7. Today, some of Andy Warhol's pieces are worth more than $100 million! _____

8. Go see Andy's artwork in person if you ever have the opportunity. _____

Identify each sentence below as simple (**S**) or compound (**C**).

1. _____ Andy sometimes told the press fictional stories about his youth.

2. _____ Andy's last name was originally Warhola, but he later changed it to Warhol.

3. _____ Andy Warhol aspired to wealth and fame.

4. _____ Andy wanted his artwork to be available to everyone, so he mass produced it.

5. _____ Did you know that Andy Warhol also produced films?

6. _____ The Factory was Andy's studio, but he also held large parties there.

7. _____ Silk screening and painting were two types of artwork Andy produced.

8. _____ Andy Warhol loved cats and created many images of them.

Review Chapter I Lessons 24–27

Review: Complex Sentences, Adjective and Adverb Clauses

Underline the dependent clause in each complex sentence below.

1. Although Tanesha lives in California, we often text each other.

2. Whenever we go to a baseball game, my dad buys us popcorn and lemonade.

3. We can visit the Empire State Building before we get together with Grandpa.

4. Unless you brought rain boots with you, we probably shouldn't go for a walk.

5. Rosie gets nervous when she has to speak in front of large groups.

6. Whether or not you've done your homework, there will be a quiz on Thursday.

7. Logan rubbed Crosby's back while the vet gave the dog a shot.

8. After Dr. Hafiz reviewed the test results, she called with the news.

Read the sentences below. Circle the adjective clauses, and underline the adverb clauses.

1. Kiwis, which are flightless birds, live in New Zealand.

2. Although he loved the Mississippi River, Mark Twain almost drowned in it as a boy.

3. Until Hurricane Katrina made landfall, no one knew what devastation the broken levees would cause.

4. For more than 2,000 years, reindeer have been domesticated.

5. The Statue of Liberty is covered in a layer of copper that is very thin.

6. Babe Ruth kept an icy cold cabbage leaf under his baseball hat during hot weather.

7. The Kingda Ka roller coaster, which is located in New Jersey, is the fastest roller coaster in North America.

8. Noah Webster, who authored the famous dictionary, attended Yale College.

Follow the directions for each item.

1. Write a complex sentence.

2. Write a sentence with an adjective clause.

_____

3. Write a compound sentence.

_____

Capitalize the first word of **every sentence**.

>*When* they are attacked, honeybees release a chemical that smells like bananas.

Capitalize the first word in **direct quotations**.

>"*Please* remember to take out the garbage," said Mom.

Do not capitalize indirect quotations.

>The coach said that the game would not be canceled.

If a continuous sentence in a direct quotation is split and the second half is not a new sentence, do not capitalize it.

>"Pack your toothbrush," said Dad, "*and* at least one change of clothes."

If a new sentence begins after the split, then capitalize it as you would any sentence.

>"I think you'll feel better soon," said Dr. Raul. "*If* you don't, please call and leave a message with the front desk."

In a letter, capitalize the name of the street, the city, the state, and the month in the heading.

>1548 *Wishing Well Lane*
>*Wichita, Kansas* 67037
>*June* 5, 2014

Capitalize the salutation, or greeting, as well as the name of the person who is receiving the letter. Capitalize the first word of the closing.

>*Dear Mr. Ball,*   *To* whom it may concern: *Your* friend,   *Sincerely,*

Rewrite It

Rewrite each sentence below using correct capitalization.

1. "what time is your swim meet this week?" asked Mom.

_____

2. "it starts at 11:00," replied Paloma, "but the coach wants us there at 10:30."

_____

3. "you need new goggles," said Mom. "the elastic on your old ones is wearing out."

_____

4. "let's wait until after the meet," said Paloma, "in case my goggles bring me good luck!"

_____

Lesson 2.1 Capitalization: Sentences, Quotations, Letter Parts

Proof It

Proofread the following letter for mistakes in capitalization. Underline a lowercase letter three times to make it a capital. m̲

office of community services
562 west bank street
springvale, vermont 05009

september 9, 2014

dear Ms. dominguez,

my family and I live in the Sardis Fields neighborhood, near the Beatty-Syms Creek. I enjoy riding my bike and hiking on the trails. however, in the last few weeks, I've been concerned by the amount of trash and litter I've noticed floating in the creek. this is hazardous to the animals that make their homes in the area. It's also bad for the environment and unpleasant for all the people who bike, hike, and walk along the creek. are there any groups who work to clean up the creek? if there are, I'd be happy to help out. If there are not, I hope your office will consider starting a group. please help make cleaning up Beatty-Syms Creek a priority in our neighborhood!

sincerely,

Alysha Piazza

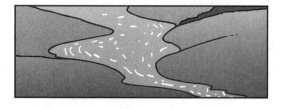

Try It

Write a dialogue between two or more people. Remember to follow the rules of capitalization.

_____

_____

_____

_____

_____

_____

Lesson 2.2 Capitalization: Names, Titles, and Places

Proper nouns are specific people, places, and things. Proper nouns are capitalized.
> The class welcomed *Oscar* by giving a standing ovation. (specific person)
> The mountains outside *Denver* glow beautifully during a sunset. (specific place)
> My favorite brand of toothpaste is *Brite White*. (specific thing)

The titles of books, poems, songs, movies, plays, newspapers, and magazines are proper nouns and are capitalized. In a title, capitalize the first and last words, and capitalize all other words except *a, an,* and *the*. Do not capitalize short prepositions, such as *of, to, in, on,* and so on. Most titles are also underlined or set in italic font in text. Song titles, essays, poems, and other shorter works are placed in quotes.
> The teacher read aloud a passage from *Little House on the Prairie*.
> Randall played "Give Peace a Chance" on the saxophone.
> An article about making cheese appeared in *Home Cooking Magazine*.
> Last weekend, we saw the classic film <u>Miracle on 34th Street</u> at a theater.

Titles associated with names are also capitalized, but do not capitalize these titles if they are not directly used with the name.
> *Mayor* Ed Koch served as *mayor* of New York City from 1978 to 1989.
> Someday, Darrell hopes to become a *professor* as talented as *Professor* Namath.

Find It
Write a complete sentence to answer each of the following questions. Be sure to capitalize any proper nouns in your answers and format titles correctly.

1. What is the title of the last movie you saw?

_____

2. What city, state, or country would you like to visit most?

_____

3. What is your favorite song or album?

_____

4. Who is the person you admire most?

_____

5. What book would you recommend for a friend to read?

_____

6. Where does the relative who lives farthest away from you live?

_____

Lesson 2.2 Capitalization: Names, Titles, and Places

Proof It
Correct the mistakes in capitalization using proofreading marks. Underline a lowercase letter three times to make it a capital. <u>m</u>

The idea that some land should be set aside for recreation began with president andrew jackson in 1832. He signed a law declaring that a hot spring in arkansas would be protected and available for use by the public. Thirty years later, abraham lincoln, who was president at the time, helped create the nation's first state park in yosemite valley, california. Eventually, the area would become yosemite national park, which is controlled by the united states government today. The honor of being the first national park, however, belongs to yellowstone national park. Located mostly in wyoming, with parts in in idaho and montana as well, yellowstone was established as a national park in march 1872 when president ulysses s. grant signed it into law.

During the next 40 years, several more national parks were established. Famous conservationist theodore roosevelt designated five more parks during his presidency. He also established the first four national monuments, which included devil's tower in wyoming. Today, 397 parks, monuments, and other sites are spread across the united states and are protected by the federal government. They even include the white house and the statue of liberty. If you want to learn more about national parks, watch ken burns's documentary *the national parks: america's best idea.*

Try It
Write a brief biography about yourself. Describe when and where you were born, who your parents or other relatives are, where your ancestors lived, where you go to school, and any other information you would like to include. Be sure to correctly capitalize proper nouns.

_____

_____

_____

_____

_____

_____

_____

_____

Lesson 2.3 Capitalization: Other Proper Nouns

Organizations, departments of government, and sections of the country are all **proper nouns** and are capitalized.

The names of organizations, associations, and businesses are capitalized.

    Carolina Waterfowl Rescue   The Rotary Club   Nike, Inc.

Capitalize the names of departments of government.

    Department of Education   Department of Homeland Security

Directional words that point out particular sections of the country are capitalized. However, words that give directions are not capitalized.

    The *West Coast* is experiencing a drought this summer.

    The ranch is located *west* of the Rockies.

Historical events, nationalities, and team names are proper nouns, as well.

Events, periods of time, and important documents from history are capitalized.

    Abigail studied the *Civil War* while in college.

Names of languages and nationalities are capitalized. They are also capitalized when they are used as adjectives.

    Raul and Donita Jiminez won the *Latin* dance competition.

The names of sports teams are capitalized.

    LeBron James left the *Cleveland Cavaliers* to play for the *Miami Heat*.

Solve It

Write a complete sentence to answer each of the following questions. Be sure to capitalize any proper nouns in your answers and to format titles correctly.

What name did Mark Twain and Charles Dudley Warner coin to describe the era in the United States spanning 1875 to 1900?

    The _____ _____ _____ _____ _____ _____ _____ _____ _____

          8   11   9   5   6   15   13 1 2

1. My grandfather worked at ___eneral ___lectric ___ompany for nearly 40 years.
                              1   2   3

2. The ___epartment of ___efense coordinates and supervises national security.
        4   5

3. We evacuated our beach house when a hurricane threatened the

    ___ast ___oast.
    6   7

4. Quinton baked a ___erman chocolate cake to bring to the potluck.
               8

5. The ___ions ___lub members rode small motorcycles in the parade.
       9   10

6. The ___ndianapolis ___olts play in the league championship this year.
     11   12

7. Ideas from the ___ge of ___nlightenment influenced the writing of the
             13   14

    ___eclaration of ___ndependence.
    15   16

Lesson 2.3 Capitalization: Other Proper Nouns

Complete It

Complete each sentence below with a proper noun. For sentences that require a specific proper noun, it is okay to write in any answer you want, but be sure you write a proper noun that fits the description and that you capitalize your answer correctly.

1. I would love to see the _Lakers_ (sports team) play the _Clippers_ (sports team).

2. The Unites States entered _____ (name of a war) after Japan attacked Pearl Harbor.

3. _____ (name of a college) is the best school in the _____ (directional word).

4. The _____ (historical document) guarantees certain freedoms for U.S. citizens.

5. During the _Civil War_ (name of a war), Abraham Lincoln gave his famous _____ (historical speech).

6. I already know how to speak _English_ (language), but someday I would love to learn _Spanish_ (language).

7. The U.S. _____ (branch of the federal government) consists of nine judges.

8. The _____ (historical period) in Europe are best known as the time of knights, peasants, and nobles.

9. The _____ (sporting event) feature events like figure skating and ski jumping.

10. Julia Child is famous for introducing _____ (nationality) cooking to Americans.

11. _Apple_ (company name) first introduced the iPod in 2001.

12. The _____ (historical period) describes the time in human history before metal tools.

13. Most of my ancestors are _____ (nationality), but I am also part _____ (nationality).

14. I am a member of _____ (name of club), and someday would also like to be a member of _____ (name of club).

15. Michael Jordan is best known for playing basketball with the _Chicago Bulls_ (sports team).

Lesson 2.4 End Marks

Periods are used at the end of declarative sentences and some imperative sentences.
Lattice encloses the garden and keeps out rabbits and deer.
Put paper in this box and cans in the other box.
Question marks are used at the end of interrogative sentences.
Where is the magnetic North Pole located?
Who sent the flowers to Ms. Mickelson?
Exclamation points are used at the end of exclamatory sentences. They are also used at the end of imperative sentences that show urgency, strong surprise, or emotion.
Mia Hamm is coming to visit our school!
Look at that eagle!

Complete It
Add an end mark to each sentence below.

1. That car just about hit Phinn _____
2. Did you see the license plate _?_
3. The car was moving too fast to read the numbers _____
4. Hand me a pencil or pen, please _____
5. I'm going to write down the make and model of the car _____
6. Do you know what model year it was _?_
7. Here comes another car going too fast _____
8. Slow down _____
9. What can be done about all these speeders _?_
10. We should write to someone in the city government _____
11. That's a great idea _____
12. Maybe the city could put a couple of speed bumps along this road _____
13. Would you help me write the letter _?_
14. Call me about it later tonight _____
15. I don't think I have your number _____
16. Write it down on that piece of paper _____
17. Hey, I just remembered something that could help us _____
18. What is it _?_
19. My cousin is good friends with the mayor's assistant _____
20. Let's call him _____

Lesson 2.4 End Marks

Identify It
Circle the end mark that correctly completes each sentence.

1. Hollywood, California, is known as the moviemaking capital of the Untied States (.) ? !)

2. Have you ever heard of Bollywood (. (?) !)

3. Bollywood is the moviemaking capital of the Indian film industry (.) ? !)

4. Do you know why it is called Bollywood (. (?) !)

5. The capital of India is Mumbai, but the city used to be called Bombay (.) ? !)

6. Bollywood gets its *B* from Bombay (. (?) !)

7. The Indian film industry releases nearly 1,000 movies each year (. ? (!)

8. That's a lot of movies (. ? (!)

9. What are *masala movies* (. (?) !)

10. Masala is a mixture of spices used in Indian cooking (.) ? !)

11. Bollywood films are known for mixing many different genres into the same movie (.) ? !)

12. A movie will have comedy, drama, singing, dancing, and action sequences (. ? (!)

13. Like spicy masala used for cooking, masala movies have many different ingredients (.) ? !)

14. With that many ingredients, masala movies often last for three hours or more (. ? (!)

15. I could never sit still so long (.) ? !)

16. The actors and actresses show their emotions through singing and dancing (.) ? !)

17. What would it be like in real life if everyone suddenly broke into song and began dancing (.) ? !)

18. Imagine the fun (. ? (!)

Try It
Write one example of each type of sentence listed below. Be sure to use the correct end mark.

Imperative sentence showing excitement or emotion: _____

_____

Declarative sentence: _____

Interrogative sentence: _____

Imperative sentence: _____

Review · Chapter 2 Lessons 1– 4

Review: Capitalization of Sentences, Quotations, Names, Titles, Places, and Other Proper Nouns; End Marks

Proofread each sentence below for capitalization. Lowercase a letter by making a slash through it M̸, and capitalize a letter by making three lines below it m̲ .

1. Kate grew up on the east coast, but after college, she moved to New Mexico.

2. "does the play start at 6 or 6:30?" asked Will. "if we leave now, we should be on time."

3. I just learned that uncle Gordon has worked for the department of health and human services for more than 20 years.

4. Vidas is lithuanian, although he doesn't speak the language.

5. Mr. Temple's first article appeared in *photography today* magazine.

6. When I visited her last Summer, my Aunt bought my favorite cereal—green earth granola.

7. To reach the wilton museum of arts and crafts, turn West on broad street.

8. Did you know that six Presidents have been named James?

9. Donita plans to be a Doctor someday, but she hasn't decided on a specialty yet.

10. "Did the water expand or contract," wondered Stuart, "After you put it in the freezer?"

11. Did you know that portuguese is the official language of brazil?

12. Ms. Malone said that If you read the materials, you shouldn't have any problems on the test.

13. Dad doesn't follow professional sports, but he's a big fan of the nebraska huskers.

14. Next year, the Khem family plans to visit grand teton national park in wyoming during summer vacation.

15. "Olivia, we just won two tickets to the Academy Awards!" Shouted Mrs. Nagy.

Review · Chapter 2 Lessons 1– 4

Review: Capitalization of Letter Parts, End Marks

Read each letter part below. If it is correct, make a check mark on the line. If it contains an error in capitalization, make an **X** on the line.

1. _____ Seattle, WA 98107

2. _____ Yours Truly,

3. _____ To Whom It May Concern:

4. _____ Mount vernon, OH 43050

5. _____ Dear davis,

6. _____ Sincerely,

7. _____ august 14, 2014

8. _____ your friend,

Add the appropriate end mark to each sentence below.

1. Spring peepers, tiny frogs, fill their vocal sacs with air that makes a sound when it is released ____

2. Wow, a hailstone can weigh more than two pounds ____

3. The presidential $1-coin program is similar to the state quarters program ____

4. Winter solstice, which is celebrated by people all over the world, is the shortest day of the year ____

5. Did you know that wildfires can create a tornado of fire called a fire whirl ____

6. The first American circus debuted in 1793 ____

7. Mariah and her sister made a gingerbread house that weighs 22 pounds ____

8. The existence of rogue waves, or freak waves, was thought to be a myth not long ago ____

9. Have you ever tried to make your own paints from natural materials ____

10. Is it true that Harriet Tubman served as a Union spy during the Civil War ____

11. Watch out for that dog ____

12. Do you know when Chinese New Year falls this year ____

13. Chop the vegetables, and then add them to the wok ____

Lesson 2.5 # Commas: Series, Direct Address, Multiple Adjectives

Series commas are used with three or more items listed in a sentence. The items can be words or phrases and are separated by commas.

> The Nile, the Amazon, and the Yangtze are among the longest rivers in the world.
> To make granola, we'll need oats, nuts, dried fruit, and honey.

Commas are used to separate the name of a person spoken to from the rest of the sentence. This is called a **direct address**.

> Sato, where did you leave your backpack?
> Thanks so much for coming, Mr. Claussen.

When **multiple adjectives** describe a noun, they are separated by commas.

> I bought the fresh, sweet cherries at the farmers' market.
> Audrey made some bright, colorful paintings for her bedroom.

Make sure the adjectives equally modify the noun. If they are coordinate adjectives, you can switch the order without changing the meaning.

> The eager, impulsive child could not wait her turn. (coordinate adjectives)
> Zane wore shiny rubber boots. (non-coordinate adjectives)

Read the sentences below. Add commas where they are needed. If the sentence is correct as it is, make a check mark on the line.

Proof It

1. _____ Owen do you know how to make your own soft pretzels?

2. _____ You'll need warm water yeast, sugar flour salt butter and an egg.

3. _____ The soft warm pretzels will taste delicious.

4. _____ Put the yeast in a bowl, add the water, and stir in the sugar.

5. _____ Please preheat the oven to 425°, Kate.

6. _____ Put the dough in a bowl cover it and allow it to rise.

7. _____ Can you wash the measuring cup, wooden spoon, and bowl Owen?

8. _____ Roll out the dough, shape it, and place it on a baking sheet.

9. _____ The salty chewy crust on the pretzels turned out perfectly.

10. _____ A glass of nice, cold iced tea would taste wonderful with the pretzels.

11. _____ Kate did you hear the timer go off?

12. _____ Grab the square red plate, and we'll take some pretzels to Louie Jake and Nadia.

Lesson 2.5 # Commas: Series, Direct Address, Multiple Adjectives

Match It
Read the sentences below. Decide what kind of comma (if any) is needed in each sentence. Write the letter of your answer on the line.

a. series comma   **b.** direct address comma
c. multiple adjectives comma   **d.** no comma needed

1. _____ The library smelled of dusty well-read old books.

2. _____ Isaiah, do you want to go to the library after school?

3. _____ Breyton likes to read mysteries science fiction and biographies.

4. _____ How long have you been a librarian Ms. Nealy?

5. _____ Many patrons like to read on the soft leather couches by the fireplace.

6. _____ If you join the summer reading club, you have the opportunity to earn stickers, pencils, CDs, and books.

7. _____ Sierra volunteers at the library on Mondays, Thursdays, and Saturdays.

8. _____ That old crumbling building at the corner used to be the town library when my grandmother was a child.

9. _____ The enormous dictionary has a decorative leather cover.

10. _____ Teddy borrowed books about Brazil, the moon, and woodworking.

Try It
For each number below, write a sentence that includes the items in parentheses.

1. (series commas and direct address)

_____

2. (multiple adjectives)

_____

3. (multiple adjectives and direct address)

_____

4. (series commas)

_____

5. (direct address)

_____

Lesson 2.6 Commas: Combining Sentences, Setting Off Dialogue

Use a comma to **combine two independent clauses** with a coordinate conjunction.
> The researcher opened the door to the cage, and a small, white mouse crawled into his hand.

In a complex sentence, **connect a dependent and an independent clause** with a comma and subordinate conjunction.
> Because Jared's glasses had broken, he was unable to take the English test.

Commas are used when **setting off dialogue** from the rest of the sentence.
> Aunt Helen replied, "I don't know if you're aware of what you're getting into!"
> "If you want to watch a movie before bed," hollered Dad, "you'll have to get started right now!"

Identify It
Read each sentence below. If it is correct, write **C** on the line. If it is incorrect, write **X** on the line and add commas where they are needed.

1. _____ India is a peninsula, which means it is surrounded by water on three sides.

2. _____ Although part of India is desert it also has jungles and mountains.

3. _____ Cows are sacred in India so Hindus do not eat beef.

4. _____ Sean asked "Did you know that the oldest Indian civilization began about 5,000 years ago?"

5. _____ Mahatma Gandhi a famous Indian pacifist was instrumental in helping India gain independence from Britain.

6. _____ "Our flight to New Delhi leaves at 8:00" began Nigel "but I'd like to be at the airport at least two hours before that."

7. _____ Because India has so many different climates, it is home to thousands of species of animals.

8. _____ "We visited many relatives on our trip to India, but we also stopped at many tourist destinations," said Sanj.

9. _____ By the mid 1750s Britain controlled much of India.

Lesson 2.6 Commas: Combining Sentences, Setting Off Dialogue

Proof It
Read the selection below. Add commas where they are needed using proofreaders' marks ⌄ . Fifteen commas are missing.

Addy walked into the kitchen where her mom was preparing a stir-fry for dinner. "Mom, have you ever heard of Hurricane Hunters?" she asked.

Mrs. Hawthorne opened a carton of mushrooms and she handed them to Addy to chop. "I think so" she responded. "I don't really know much about them, though."

"We watched a documentary about them in science today and I think I want to be one!" exclaimed Addy, scraping the mushroom into the wok. "I've thought about joining the Air Force after high school and I love science. I think it would be a perfect career for me."

"Tell me more about them" said Mrs. Hawthorne. "I'm not sure exactly what Hurricane Hunters do."

Addy stirred the vegetables. "Hurricane Hunters fly right into the eye of a hurricane where they gather data about the storm. They measure wind speed and they look for the pressure center. The data they send back can help forecasters do their job."

"It sounds so interesting, Addy" said her mom "but it also sounds incredibly dangerous."

Addy smiled and replied "I knew you'd say that so I'm prepared. Although it is a dangerous job they've flown over 100,000 hours without a problem!"

"Oh, Addy" sighed Mrs. Hawthorne "you've always been a daredevil."

Try It
Write a short dialogue between yourself and a family member. Remember to use commas correctly in your writing.

_____

_____

_____

_____

_____

_____

Lesson 2.7 Commas: Personal Letters and Business Letters

Commas are used in both **personal** and **business letters**.

Personal Letters

Commas appear in four of the five parts of the personal letter.

Heading:	15228 River Rock Ave.
	Santa Fe, NM 87004
	February 27, 2014
Salutation:	Dear Pilar,
Body:	comma usage in sentences
Closing:	Yours truly,

Business Letters

Commas appear in four of the six parts of the business letter.

Heading:	601 Dillingham Ct.
	St. Paul, MN 55108
	July 18, 2014
Inside Address:	Dr. Clare Yoshida
	Four Oaks Medical Center
	1189 Hampton Rd.
	Hartford, CT 06103
Body:	comma usage in sentences
Closing:	Sincerely,

Rewrite It

Rewrite each item below. Include commas where they are needed.

1. Your friend _____

2. April 14 1809 _____

3. My degree is in marketing and I have had several internships.

_____

4. Regards _____

5. San Rafael CA 94903 _____

6. We visited the botanical gardens the planetarium and the art museum.

_____

7. Dear Grandma Suzanne _____

8. All my best _____

9. August 11 2014 _____

10. Rock Hill SC 29732 _____

Lesson 2.7 | # Commas: Personal Letters and Business Letters

Proof It

Read the letter below and look for places where commas are missing. Use proofreaders' marks ⌄ to add the missing commas.

557 West Mound St.
Madison WI 53532
October 21 2014

Mr. George Cohen
Oakvale Public Library
1862 Lincoln Ln.
Madison WI 53532

Dear Mr. Cohen:

My name is Elizabeth Yang and I'm a seventh grade student at Roosevelt Middle School. I'm interested in becoming a volunteer at Oakvale Library. I know that many of your volunteers reshelve books. I would enjoy shelving books but I'm also interested in working in the children's section. Perhaps I could help the children's librarian with story time? I love spending time with children and I attended story time myself until I started elementary school. I have worked as a mother's helper for the last two summers so I have quite a bit of experience working with young children. I have been an avid reader since I was five. I still remember many of my favorite books from that time!

I would be available on Wednesdays after school and on Sunday afternoons. I look forward to speaking with you about volunteer opportunities at the library.
Thank you for your time and consideration.

Sincerely
Elizabeth A. Yang
Elizabeth A. Yang

Try It

Write a letter to a friend or family member. Remember to use commas where needed, including in the body of the letter.

_____

_____

_____

_____

_____

Lesson 2.8 Semicolons and Colons

Colons have several functions in a sentence.

Colons are used to introduce a series in a sentence. Colons are not needed when the series is preceded by a verb or preposition.

> The Massey Glee Club performed in the following cities: *Roanoke, Danville,* and *Blacksburg.*
>
> The flavors offered at the ice cream shop are chocolate, vanilla, and strawberry. (no colon needed)

Colons are sometimes used instead of a comma to set off a clause.

> Maestro Bing told the orchestra: *"The third movement must be flawless."*

Colons are used to set off a word or phrase for emphasis.

> Shawn's knees shook as he realized who was at the door: *Principal Nelson.*

Colons are used when writing the time.

> We need to be waiting outside the station by *10:00.*

Business letters use colons in the salutation. *Dear Sir or Madam*:

A **semicolon** is a cross between a period and a comma.

Semicolons join two independent clauses when a coordinate conjunction is not used.

> Bats are hibernating in the vents of my attic; they will need to be relocated in the spring.

Semicolons are used to separate clauses when they already contain commas.

> Late at night, I heard cars honking, people yelling, and sirens blaring; which is why I cannot sleep.

Semicolons are also used to separate series of words or phrases that already contain commas.

> Students in Mr. Hirochi's class measured, marked, and cut the cloth into pieces; sewed the pieces together in a pattern; and then displayed the finished quilt on the front wall.

Rewrite It

Rewrite the following sentences, adding colons or semicolons where needed.

1. Snow fell throughout the night by morning, the drifts were two feet high.

_____

2. Please pick up the following items at the store a hairbrush, toothpaste, three bars of soap, and a bottle of lotion.

_____

3. This morning I downloaded apps for my MP3 player, phone, and tablet I walked the dog to the park and back and I cleaned out my car.

_____

4. At the post office this morning, you won't believe who I saw Jude Law.

_____

Lesson 2.8 Semicolons and Colons

Proof It
In the sentences below, colons and semicolons are missing or used incorrectly. Correct each sentence by adding, replacing, or deleting colons and semicolons as needed.

1. The string quartet consists of: a cello, a viola, and two violins.

2. The two violinists practice together every other day they are determined to make no mistakes at the concert.

3. The cellist, Henry Warner, gets up very early to practice each morning 400 A.M.!

4. At the last concert, right in the middle of a song, a string broke on Helen's viola: but as she replaced it, the audience waited patiently.

5. At each performance, Helen wears a black dress, high heels, and a lucky brooch, she wishes her fellow musicians a good show, and she calls her mother afterward.

6. These venues will host their next three concerts, Royal Music Hall, Lakeside Auditorium, and the Bentley Music Center.

7 Cellos are bigger than violins, they also produce a deeper sound.

8. Henry reminded Helen; "Make sure you have new strings on your viola."

9. The concert at the Royal Music Hall is scheduled to begin at 730.

10. The first violist to join the quartet was Janice Stringer, Molly Hills joined second.

11. The quartet will play pieces by: Beethoven, Mozart, and Brahms.

12. Although the Beethoven piece is rather difficult, Helen had played it before, so when the quartet first practiced it, she helped teach the others.

13. The quartet decided to include one piece as a surprise for the audience, Bob Dylan's "All Along the Watchtower."

14. Three special guests attended the performance; Mayor Hank Satterly, Professor Mia Ling, and the well-known cellist Yo-Yo Ma.

15. The quartet strode onstage, the audience erupted with applause.

16. After the players sat down, they took a moment to tune their instruments, and then after a brief pause, they launched into the first song.

17. The four bows swept across, jumped over, and sawed against the strings: the music filled the concert hall: and the audience basked in the beauty.

18. Mingled with the applause that followed, one word rang out from different parts of the hall "Bravo!"

Lesson 2.9 Quotation Marks

Quotation marks are used to show the exact words of a speaker. The quotation marks are placed before and after the exact words.

> *"Did you bring flowers for Alice?" asked Carl. "Her party starts in about an hour."*

Quotation marks are also used when a direct quotation contains another direct quotation.

> Hector explained, *"Beth said, 'Take the train, or you'll get stuck in traffic.'"*

Note that single quotation marks are used to set off the inside quotation. Single quotes express what Beth said. Double quotes express what Hector said.

Quotation marks are used with some titles. Quotation marks are used with the titles of short stories, poems, songs, and articles in magazines and newspapers.

> My favorite poem in A. A. Milne's *When We Were Very Young* is "At the Zoo."

If a title is quoted within a direct quotation, then single quotation marks are used.

> Melinda asked, "Have you read 'Flight' by John Steinbeck?"

Complete It
Add double or single quotation marks where they are needed in each sentence.

1. We need to determine how many ducks arrived at the pond yesterday, Dr. Steinberg explained.

2. Lotta reassured the others when she said, Mr. Yates said, Don't worry if the experiment fails the first time. So we just need to try again.

3. My favorite song of all time is Yellow Submarine by The Beatles, said Laura.

4. We should probably get going, said Dawna. The doctor said, Arrive fifteen minutes early to fill out some paperwork before your exam.

5. Our neighbors, the Worths, are installing a pool, said Mia.

6. After his sister recited some of The Rime of the Ancient Mariner, Noah asked, You don't have to memorize the whole poem do you?

7. The title of my essay is What's Next for Staunton? the mayor explained.

8. How much money did you bring? Jessie asked. The tickets are almost $20 apiece.

9. Before Katie left on the trip, she read an article entitled Don't Get Lost: Ten Tips for Using a Compass.

10. As Lucas studied the image, he remembered what his teacher had said: A skull is usually a symbol for mortality.

Lesson 2.9 Quotation Marks

Proof It

The passage below contains several errors with quotation marks. Edit the passage to correct the mistakes.

Ms. Langstrom said, 'For the next couple of weeks, we will be reading short stories and poems by author and poet Gary Soto. "Has anyone read his work before?'

Katie raised her hand and replied, 'Last year at my old school, we read most of *Baseball in April and Other Stories*. My favorite story was La Bamba.'

Today, I will read the poem Ode to Family Photographs, Ms. Langstrom explained.

As she read aloud, Luis whispered to Katie, 'One time my dad said, Poems are like X-rays of the world. I've always remembered that.

Luis looked up. Ms. Langstrom had stopped reading and was staring at him. "Do you have something to share with us, Luis?

I'm sorry, Ms. Langstrom. I was telling Katie something my dad once said. He described poems as being "like X-rays of the world."

That's a nice simile, Luis, Ms. Langstrom agreed, but I wish you'd wait until I'm done reading to talk about it.

"Yes, Ma'am, replied Luis.

Ms. Langstrom finished the reading. Then, she asked the students to name other poems they knew.

'I Wandered Lonely as a Cloud is the only poem I can name," admitted Kieran.

That's the famous first line of Wordsworth's Daffodils, Kieran, Ms. Langstrom clarified. But it's not the title.

The teacher began handing out copies of *Baseball in April*. "Everybody, please read the story Broken Chain by Wednesday. Then, she smiled at Katie and added, This should mostly be a review for you, Katie, so I expect good work.

Try It

Write a short dialogue between two friends discussing their favorite songs. Be sure to use single and double quotes where they are needed.

_____

_____

_____

_____

_____

_____

_____

_____

Lesson 2.10 Using Italics and Underlining

When you are working on a computer, use **italics** for the titles of books, plays, movies, television series, magazines, and newspapers. If you are writing by hand, **underline** these titles.

Pride and Prejudice is my favorite book, as well as my mother's. (book)
Maxwell's parents have a subscription to *The New York Times*. (newspaper)
Serena loves to watch the show *Bizarre Foods* with her brothers. (TV show)

Identify It
Underline the title or titles in each sentence that should be italicized.

1. Micah enjoys learning about science and nature, so his grandpa got him a subscription to Odyssey magazine.

2. The Boy Who Dared is a fictional book about World War II and Hitler's rise to power.

3. Everyone in my family enjoys watching the show Modern Family.

4. Tiana and her parents are going to see a production of Shakespeare's A Midsummer Night's Dream at a park downtown.

5. Eli is writing a research paper about Ruby Bridges, so he borrowed the book Through My Eyes from the library.

6. Julia loved the movie Little Women as much as she loved the book.

7 Have you read Does My Head Look Big in This by Randa Abdel-Fattah?

8. If you like adventure stories, you must read the book Raft by Stephanie Bodeen.

9. I need to find the article about the current bee crisis that was in last Sunday's Washington Post.

10. My school is going to be putting on the play Alice, which is based on Lewis Carroll's famous book, Alice's Adventures in Wonderland.

11. On Saturday, Jian went to the 3:00 showing of The Watsons Go to Birmingham.

12. Carrie's photo was in the Arts section of the Kansas City Star!

13. The school library has hundreds of copies of National Geographic.

14. My favorite episode of Survivorman takes place in the Arctic.

Lesson 2.10 Using Italics and Underlining

Try It

Answer each of the following questions with a complete sentence.

1. What book have you read recently that you would recommend to a friend?

   _____

2. What is the name of a movie you've seen that that is based on a book?

   _____

3. What magazine have you used as a source for a school paper or essay?

   _____

4. If you could go to New York City and see a play performed on Broadway, what would it be?

   _____

5. What is the title of a book you've read (or would like to read) more than once?

   _____

6. What is the name of your hometown newspaper?

   _____

7. If you could get a free subscription to a magazine, which magazine would it be?

   _____

8. What television show would you recommend to your best friend?

   _____

9. What was your favorite movie when you were in first grade?

   _____

10. Have you ever quit reading or watching in the middle of a book or a movie? What was it called?

   _____

Lesson 2.11 Apostrophes

Apostrophes are used in contractions, to form possessives, and to form plurals. Apostrophes take the place of the omitted letters in contractions.
          we will = we'll   would not = wouldn't

Possessives show possession, or ownership. To form the possessive of a singular noun, add an apostrophe and an *s*. This rule applies even if the noun already ends in *s*.
          The koala**'s** fur was thick and soft.   Is that Charle**s's** car?

To form the possessive of plural nouns ending in *s*, add an apostrophe. If the plural noun does not end in *s*, add both the apostrophe and an *s*.
          The chef**s'** opinions about the new restaurant appear in the review.
          The children**'s** boots are lined up by the door.

Identify It
Read each sentence below. If the apostrophes are used correctly, make a check mark on the line. If they are used incorrectly or are missing, make an **X** on the line.

1. _____ Karim's yoga class meets at 4:00 on Wednesday afternoon.

2. _____ The girls running club was started by Missy Polaski and Anya Padma.

3. _____ As the buzzer rang, we could hear the parents cheers echoing through the stadium.

4. _____ Serenity should'nt miss volleyball practice again this week.

5. _____ Mattys' hiking club is planning to walk a section of the Appalachian Trail this weekend.

6. _____ The year-end party for the lacrosse team is going to be held at the Baxters' house.

7. _____ Reggie cant play baseball again until his ankle is fully healed.

8. _____ In spite of the students' cheers, Liam was able to focus on the ball and make a final goal.

9. _____ Although the coaches' voice was calm, we could tell how excited he was.

10. _____ After an especially long swim practice, Selena's eyes were burning.

11. _____ Camerons' skis and poles were stolen last week!

12. _____ We'll pick you up after your track meet.

13. _____ The Yellowjackets scored as a result of the quarterbacks' great throw.

14. _____ Holly and Noah won't admit that the loss wasn't their fault.

15. _____ The Lakeshore Womens' Rowing Club is sponsoring the school's rowing team this year.

Lesson 2.11 Apostrophes

Proof It
Each sentence below is missing at least one apostrophe. Add the apostrophes where they are needed using this proofreading mark ⌄ .

1. Cows manure is used as fertilizer on farms all across America.

2. What you probably didnt know, though, is that manure can be used to create power.

3. A single cow can produce about 30 gallons of manure a day—its easy to see how much an entire dairy farm could produce!

4. Scientists solution for dealing with all that manure is to turn it into power.

5. A giant scooper cleans a barns floor of manure.

6. The manures placed in a giant tank called a digester.

7. The digesters job is similar to the job that occurs in a cows stomach.

8. If a farmers crops don't do well one year, its nice to have another source of income.

9. Another benefit of cow manure energy is that it isnt a fossil fuel.

10. The USDAs Rural Energy for America program provides grants to Iowas famers.

11. Utility companies need to be willing to buy farmers manure energy.

12. Liquid that is a byproduct of the digester is used as fertilizer and surprisingly doesnt smell at all!

Try It
On the lines below, write two sentences that include contractions and two that include possessives.

_____

_____

_____

_____

Lesson 2.12 Hyphens, Dashes, and Parentheses

Hyphens are used to divide words that come at the end of a line. Divide words between syllables.

> Bradford Landscaping lined our driveway with monkey grasses and orna–mental flowering plants.

Do not divide one letter from the rest of the word, and divide syllables after the vowel if the vowel is a syllable by itself. Divide words with double consonants between the consonants.

> associa-tion, not a-ssociation or associ-ation
> hum-ming   mid-dle

Hyphens are used between compound numbers from twenty-one through ninety-nine.

> Only *twenty-seven* of the class's *thirty-one* students attended the science fair.

Hyphens are used in compound modifiers only when the modifier precedes the word it modifies. Hyphens are not used for compound modifiers that include adverbs ending in *-ly*.

> I presented a *well-researched* report to the board. My report was well researched.
> Even a *carefully built* sandcastle will collapse eventually.

Use hyphens in some compound nouns. You will need to check in a dictionary to be sure which compound nouns need hyphens.

> Mari and Lexi stood in line for a ride on the *merry-go-round*.

Dashes indicate a sudden break or a change in thought.

> We took our rabbit—her name is Lily—outside to run around in the backyard.

Parentheses show supplementary, or additional, material or set off phrases in a stronger way than commas.

> On the second Wednesday of next month (*March 12*) we will host a formal tea party.
> Sunlight coming in the windows (*the windows at the front of the house*) has faded one side of our couch.

Complete It
Add hyphens where they are needed in the following sentences. Use a dictionary if you need help.

1. My mother in law, Mildred, is a self taught artist.

2. She has twenty five beautifully painted landscapes that are all well protected in side a leather portfolio.

3. Her first born child is my wife, Nancy.

4. Mildred thought painting was a long lost skill, but she was pleasantly sur prised to discover she was still a highly talented artist.

5. Recently, she had a well attended exhibition at a locally owned gallery.

Lesson 2.12 Hyphens, Dashes, and Parentheses

Rewrite It
Rewrite the following sentences, adding parentheses, dashes, and hyphens where needed.

1. My great aunt visits us every Sunday even if there's a blizzard so we can cook together.

_____

2. We use a well worn cookbook it was originally my great great grandmother's that contains about fifty five different recipes.

_____

3. During the below freezing days of winter, we prefer cooking a belly warming pot of stew or soup.

_____

4. My not so patient younger brother his name is Eli mills around while we cook, trying to snatch samples what a pest!

_____

5. Chopping onions is an eye stinging chore my eyes water and my nose runs, but I don't mind doing it.

_____

6. Great Aunt Ruth handles the dangerously hot boiling broth we use organic chicken broth.

_____

7. In summer, we cook with farm fresh vegetables bought at the farmer's market Saturday is market day.

_____

8. During the winter, our well stocked grocery store it's just a few blocks from our house provides the ingredients we need.

_____

Try It
Write three sentences below: one with a hyphen, one with a dash, and one with parentheses.

1. _____

2. _____

3. _____

Review: Commas, Colons, and Semicolons

The letter below is missing all of its commas. Add commas where they are needed.

1352 Basin Ave.
Harrisburg PA 32654
May 22 2015

Mr. Louis Randolph
541 East 12th Street
Philadelphia PA 34115

Dear Mr. Randolph:

Thank you so much for your donation! The lions panthers and other big cats at our preserve will greatly benefit from your generous gift. Although thousands of visitors pay an admission fee each year it is rare for us to receive a direct donation like the one you have provided Louis. Please know that you are welcome any time to visit the preserve free of charge and we encourage you to bring guests as well. When you come to the preserve next time you will get a chance to visit our new visitor center. A large colorful mural was painted inside and it shows our beloved cats in their natural environments. It was largely thanks to you Louis that we were able to complete the project.

Sincerely
Meredith Sanchez

Each sentence below is missing a comma, colon, or semicolon. On the line, write in the appropriate punctuation mark.

1. Please provide one of the following pieces of identification___ a drivers license, a passport, or another type of photo ID.

2. We were headed to the bank___ but then I realized I had forgotten my wallet.

3. You won't believe the new animal they have at the zoo___a wombat!

4. Manny's boots were just a little too big___ he had several blisters by the end of the hike.

5. When Lucy gets home from school___ she will need to practice piano.

6. Before I left for work, I placed a sandwich in my briefcase___ but by lunchtime, the sandwich was missing.

Review   Chapter 2 Lessons 5–12

Review: Quotation Marks, Using Italics and Underlining, Apostrophes, Hyphens, Dashes, and Parentheses

Rewrite each sentence below to add quotation marks or apostrophes where they are needed. Two sentences also contain words that need to be underlined when you rewrite the sentences.

I. How many students will be attending the Fun Fair? asked Ms. Pings assistant.

_____

2. Ill make sure you get the credit youve earned, said Marci.

_____

3. Alexander told his friends about Tysons notebook getting stolen.

_____

4. The mountains peak looks brilliant in this light, explained Harlan, which is why I love this time of day.

_____

5. My favorite of Ibsens plays is A Dolls House, Mr. Conrad said to a students mother.

_____

6. My aunts friend Timothy said, At tomorrows Arbor Day celebration, I will read aloud the poem Trees.

_____

7. Bess agreed with her classmates, exclaiming, I love the movie Star Wars too!

_____

8. Walt said, I heard the mailman say, The Wilsons vacation ended early because of rain.

_____

Add hyphens where they are needed in each sentence below.

I. Dr. Manuel presented a well reasoned argument to the board of directors.

2. I received a jack in the box for my fifty seventh birthday; a middle aged man is much too old for such a gift!

3. After the first string running back fumbled, the highly disappointed fans groaned.

Chapter 3 Usage
Lesson 3.1 Word Roots

The **root** of a word is the main part of the word. It tells the main meaning, and other word parts add to the main meaning.

The root *port* means "to carry."
The word *import* means "to carry in."
The word *portable* means "can be carried."

If an unfamiliar word contains a familiar root, knowing the meaning of the root can give you a clue to the meaning of the unfamiliar word.

A **base word** is a root that is a complete word.

The base word of *reacted* is *act*.

Identify It
On the line, write an example of another word that contains the same root or base word that has been underlined. Use a dictionary if you need help.

1. pre<u>dict</u> _____

2. de<u>funct</u> _____

3. <u>spect</u>acles _____

4. re<u>serve</u> _____

5. incap<u>able</u> _____

6. con<u>struct</u>ion _____

7. autobio<u>graphy</u> _____

8. <u>erupt</u>ing _____

9. tri<u>cycle</u> _____

10. manu<u>facture</u> _____

11. in<u>form</u>ation _____

12. in<u>numer</u>able _____

13. <u>photo</u>synthesis _____

14. tele<u>phone</u> _____

15. <u>trans</u>portation _____

16. re<u>wind</u> _____

17. unre<u>cogn</u>izable _____

18. <u>sens</u>ation _____

19. e<u>vol</u>ution _____

20. e<u>va</u>cuate _____

Lesson 3.1 Word Roots

Match each root in Column A with its meaning in Column B. Use a dictionary if you need help.

Column A	**Column B**
fort as in *fortitude*	free
path as in *sympathy*	bend
struct as in *construct*	breath
liber as in *liberty*	see
flect as in *reflection*	change
pac as in *pacify*	build
spir as in *respiration*	strength
gen as in *generation*	peace
vid as in *video*	feeling
vert as in *convert*	birth

Try It

Choose five roots from the list above. Think of a word other than the one shown for each root and use it in a sentence. Write your sentences on the lines below.

1. root: _____ sentence:_____

_____

2. root: _____ sentence:_____

_____

3. root: _____ sentence:_____

_____

4. root: _____ sentence:_____

_____

5. root: _____ sentence:_____

_____

Lesson 3.2 Prefixes and Suffixes

Prefixes and suffixes change the meanings of root and base words. A **prefix** is a word part added to the beginning of a root or base word. For example, the prefix *un-* means "not" or "opposite," so *unequal* means "**not** equal."

Some common prefixes and their meanings are listed below.

in-, im-, ir-, il- = "not"	irregular, impolite
re- = "again"	refreeze
dis- = "not, opposite of"	disconnect
non- = "not"	nonslip
over- = "too much"	overcook
mis- = "wrongly"	miscalculate
pre- = "before"	precut
inter- = "between, among"	intercoastal

Match It

Write a word in the blank that matches each definition below. The word should contain a prefix and a base word found in the definition.

1. not cooked _____

2. to understand wrongly _____

3. appear again _____

4. not visible _____

5. load too much _____

6. discover again _____

7. to diagnose wrongly _____

8. not married _____

9. to qualify before _____

10. not mature _____

11. the opposite of approve _____

12. not living _____

13. slept too much _____

14. between states _____

Lesson 3.2 Prefixes and Suffixes

A **suffix** is a word part added to the end of a root or base word. Sometimes, the spelling of the root or base word changes when a suffix is added. For example, the suffix –*ness* means "state or condition of." *Happiness* means "the state or condition of being happy." Note that the final –*y* in *happy* changes to *i* before adding the suffix.

Some common suffixes and their meanings are listed below.

–*ful* = "characterized by or tending to"	playful
–*y* = "characteristic of"	angrily
–*er*, –*or* = "one who" or "person connected with"	dreamer
–*on*, –*tion*, –*ation*, –*ition* = "act or process"	animation
–*ic* = "having characteristics of"	allergic
–*less* = "without"	harmless
–*en* = "made of" or "to make"	brighten

Solve It
Read each definition below. Fill in the correct space in the crossword puzzle with a word that ends in a suffix and matches the definition.

Across

  1. without pain

  4. act or process of competing

  6. to make dark

  7. characterized by beauty

  9. to make thick

  10. characterized by joy

Down

  2. the state or condition of being shy

  3. having characteristics of science

  5. act or process of investigating

  8. characteristic of history

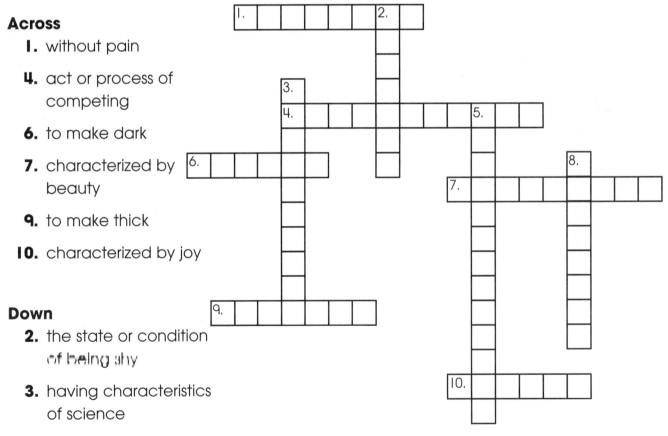

Lesson 3.2 Prefixes and Suffixes

Complete It
Complete each sentence below with a simple definition for the word shown in italics. Use the root of the word as part of your definition where you can. Then, underline the word's prefix or suffix. Use a dictionary if you need help.

1. Someone who is *disloyal* is _____.

2. A *surveyor* is _____.

3. If you *predict* an event that happens, you _____.

4. I *overestimated* the cost of the meal, meaning I _____.

5. To *transfer* money from a savings account to a checking account means _____ .

6. A *worthy* opponent is an opponent who _____.

7. A building under *construction* is _____.

8. If you are *flexible*, then you _____.

9. An *incorrect* answer on a quiz is _____.

10. Cooks often prefer *nonstick* pans because _____.

Try It
On each line below, write a sentence that includes a word with the prefix or suffix indicated.

1. the suffix *–ful*

_____

2. the prefix *un–*

_____

3. the prefix *re–*

_____

4. the suffix *–er*

_____

5. the prefix *dis–*

_____

6. the prefix *pre–*

_____

Lesson 3.2 Prefixes and Suffixes

Identify It

Identify twelve words in the passage below that contain a prefix, a suffix, or both a prefix and a suffix. Use the lines below to identify the different words parts. Some words may have more than one suffix. One example has been provided.

A rat quickly scurries across the jungle floor. Nearby, a predator lies patiently in the dense underbrush, soundless and still. Suddenly, more than 10 feet of solid muscular power launches at the rat, and in an instant, the rat is in the attacker's mouth. This predator is a boa <u>constrictor</u>, but it isn't ready to eat yet. These snakes are not venomous—their bites are not deadly—and swallowing the animal alive would be foolish and harmful. A live rat would scratch and bite the snake's insides. Instead, the boa uses its powerful body to squeeze the rat and restrict airflow into its lungs. Soon, respiration ceases, and the boa can swallow its prey safely. Boas have stretchy tissue connecting their jaws, so they can open their jaws extremely wide, enabling them to swallow animals of various sizes. The rat, like all of the boa's prey, is swallowed whole. Digestion occurs as the rat works its way through the snake's body. After consuming a sufficiently large meal, a snake might not require additional food for several weeks. Satisfied with its rat snack, this boa is ready to retire for the evening.

Prefix	**Root**	**Suffix**
1. *con*	*strict*	*or*
2. _____	_____	_____
3. _____	_____	_____
4. _____	_____	_____
5. _____	_____	_____
6. _____	_____	_____
7. _____	_____	_____
8. _____	_____	_____
9. _____	_____	_____
10. _____	_____	_____
11. _____	_____	_____
12. _____	_____	_____

Try It

Using the root word *form*, add prefixes and suffixes to create new words. How many different words can you create? Write them on the lines below.

_____

_____

Lesson 3.3 Double Negatives

Double negatives occur when two negative words are used in the same sentence. Negative words include *not, no, never, nobody, nowhere, nothing, barely, hardly, scarcely,* and contractions containing the word *not.* Avoid using double negatives—they are grammatically incorrect.

To correct a double negative, you can delete one of the negative words or replace it with an affirmative, or positive, word. Affirmative words are the opposite of negative words. Examples include *some, somewhere, someone, anyone, any,* and *always.*

Negative: Mr. Zingale *can't* do anything until Ava's parents arrive.
Double Negative: Mr. Zingale *can't* do *nothing* until Ava's parents arrive.

Negative: *Don't* use any slang in your e-mail to Ms. Sanchez.
Double Negative: *Don't* use *no* slang in your e-mail to Ms. Sanchez.

Complete It
Underline the word or words in parentheses that best complete each sentence below.

1. Because of the icy runway, the airplane couldn't go (nowhere, anywhere).

2. Sullivan doesn't think that (nobody, anyone) is going to come to his play because of the storm.

3. We hoped to receive extra credit for the handout we made for our presentation, but we didn't get (any, none).

4. Aunt Kat could barely see (anything, nothing) through the heavy downpour.

5. Isis won't (ever, never) finish his book report unless he gets some quiet time to work.

6. Lauren does not have (no, any) air in her bike tires.

7. Our ancient tabby cat, Miss Pibbles, hardly (never, ever) eats all her canned food.

8. Carson (can, can't) never contain his excitement when they arrive at the beach.

9. Although he was here for two hours, the plumber didn't do (nothing, anything) about the leak under the kitchen sink.

10. Deepak hardly missed (any, no) classes this semester.

11. Nobody (can, can't) grow juicy, red tomatoes better than my dad.

12. Julian drove around for 15 minutes, but couldn't find (nowhere, anywhere) to park.

13. The police officer won't have (no, any) back-up until her partner arrives at 9:00.

14. The bear and her cub scarcely (ever, never) come into town in the summer.

Lesson 3.3 Double Negatives

Rewrite It
Each sentence below contains a double negative. Rewrite the sentences to eliminate the double negatives. There may be more than one correct answer for each item.

1. The birds wouldn't eat none of the new birdseed.

_____

2. Don't nobody touch the wet paint on the fence!

_____

3. Ian was sleeping so deeply that he didn't hardly hear the fire alarm go off.

_____

4. The swim team wasn't interested in nothing but practicing the day before the meet.

_____

5. The Girl Scouts are not going nowhere this weekend.

_____

6. Nobody can't join the club without a unanimous vote.

_____

7. Madison hasn't never traveled outside of the United States.

_____

8. The Johannsens didn't remember to do nothing about the broken gate.

_____

Try It
Write three sentences using double negatives.

1. _____

_____

2. _____

_____

3. _____

_____

Lesson 3.4 Synonyms and Antonyms

Synonyms are words that have the same, or almost the same, meaning. Using synonyms can help you avoid repeating words and can make your writing more interesting. A thesaurus, either in book form or online, is a good source for finding synonyms.

> trash/garbage   accomplish/achieve   raise/ lift   empty/vacant

Antonyms are words that have opposite meanings. A dictionary, either in book form or online, is a good source for finding antonyms.

> attract/repel   accept/decline   cause/effect   common/rare

Rewrite It

Rewrite each sentence below. Use a synonym for **boldface** words and an antonym for underlined words.

I. Is that a **genuine** piece of turquoise?

_____

2. There is no doubt in my mind that the defendant is guilty.

_____

3. It wouldn't be difficult for me to read the text if you could **magnify** it.

_____

4. The security guard **examined** the bags before she **allowed** the couple through the gates.

_____

5. What kind of **occupation** are you interested in pursuing?

_____

6. Although I have **searched**, I cannot find a solution.

_____

7. This year, David hopes to decrease the amount of sugar he **consumes**.

_____

8. We need to stake the sapling so that its trunk will **remain** straight.

_____

9. Will the Coast Guard be able to **rescue** the passengers on the boat?

_____

Lesson 3.4 Synonyms and Antonyms

Match It
Draw a line to match each word in column A with its synonym in column B. Then, draw a line to match each word in column C with its antonym in column D.

A	B	C	D
assist	dependable	north	past
bother	gather	certain	specific
lucky	instructions	shiny	destroy
order	fortunate	fire	invisible
faithful	help	unusual	south
reliable	loyal	general	doubtful
last	sequence	future	common
directions	final	visible	hire
collect	annoy	create	dull

Find It
Use a dictionary, thesaurus, or online resource to find the following synonyms or antonyms.

I. an antonym for *accept* _____

2. a synonym for *burglar* _____

3. a synonym for *exhausted* _____

4. an antonym for *anticipate* _____

5. an antonym for *artificial* _____

6. a synonym for *conclusion* _____

7. an antonym for *careful* _____

8. a synonym for *component* _____

Lesson 3.5 Analogies

An **analogy** is a comparison between two pairs of words. To complete an analogy, figure out how the pairs of words are related.

Forest is to tree as beach is to sand.
A forest consists of trees, just as a beach consists of sand.

Leap is to jump as soar is to fly.
Leap is a synonym for jump, just as soar is a synonym for fly.

Lens is to camera as page is to book.
A lens is part of a camera, just as a page is part of a book.

Analogies are often presented without using the phrase is to and the word as. Instead, colons are used in place of is to, and two colons are used in place of as to separate the pairs being compared.

Movie is to DVD as album is to CD.
movie : DVD : : album : CD

Complete It
Circle the letter of the word that best completes each analogy.

1. ice : water : : candle : _____

    a. light   b. fire   c. wax   d. heat

2. tree : bark : : fish : _____

    a. ocean   b. scales   c. water   d. fin

3. _____ : canoe : : bus : bicycle

    a. rowboat   b. kayak   c. speedboat   d. ocean liner

4. recipe : cooking : : _____ : traveling

    a. map   b. tickets   c. airplane   d. restaurant

5. form : information : : act : _____

    a. directions   b. inaction   c. technology   d. play

6. paper : scissors : : rock : _____

    a. chisel   b. sharp   c. solid   d. gravel

7. mountain : _____ : : exterior : interior

    a. cliff   b. peak   c. ocean   d. valley

8. _____ : blades : : car : wheel

    a. knife   b. fan   c. wind   d. electricity

Lesson 3.5 Analogies

Solve It

To solve each analogy below, unscramble the word in parentheses and write it on the line.

1. *Rays* are to *sun* as _____ are to *flower*. (ptales)

2. *Herd* is to *cattle* as *pack* is to _____. (slvewo)

3. *Kangaroo* is to _____ as *frog* is to *amphibian*. (mlmama)

4. *Sunday* is to *sundae* as *raze* is to _____. (iaers)

5. *Three* is to *nine* as _____ is to *one-hundred forty-four*. (etvlew)

6. *Blunt* is to _____ as *bitter* is to *sweet*. (aphrs)

7. _____ is to *heat* as *impolite* is to *polite*. (tpaeher)

8. *Key* is to *piano* as *string* is to _____. (itagru)

9. *Squabble* is to _____ as *plummet* is to *fall*. (regua)

10. *Scale* is to *weight* as _____ is to *temperature*. (etrtmehmoer)

Try It

Follow the directions to write your own analogies.

1. Write an analogy in which the words are antonyms.

_____

2. Write an analogy that shows a grammatical relationship.

_____

3. Write an analogy that shows a numerical relationship.

_____

4. Write an analogy that shows a part-to-whole relationship.

_____

5. Write an analogy that shows an object-use relationship.

_____

6. Write an analogy in which the words are synonyms.

_____

Review Chapter 3 Lessons 1–5

Review: Word Roots, Previews and Suffixes, Negatives and Double Negatives

For each suffix or prefix, locate its meaning in the box. Write the meaning on the first line, and then write an example of a word that uses the prefix or suffix on the second line.

wrongly	act or process	one who	characterized by or tending to
made of or to make	not or opposite of	again	without

1. –er _____ _____

2. re– _____ _____

3. –en _____ _____

4. –ful _____ _____

5. mis– _____ _____

6. –less _____ _____

7. –tion _____ _____

8. dis– _____ _____

Each sentence below contains a root or base word with a familiar prefix or suffix. Underline the root or base word and circle the familiar prefix or suffix. (Each root or base word, prefix, and suffix was used in a previous lesson.)

1. Dr. Nelson checks my respiration during my medical exam.

2. Emmanuel hasn't never made a correct prediction about who will win a football game.

3. Reformers worked hard to convince the city council to change its mind.

4. A peaceful breeze drifted over my face.

5. We were misinformed about the starting time and arrived late.

6. Sam sprinkled paprika liberally onto the casserole.

7. Please don't interrupt the band while they practice.

8. A starfish can regenerate an arm if one is lost.

9. Spectators stood in the stands and cheered.

One of the sentences above contains a double negative. Identify the sentence and then rewrite it correctly below.

_____

Review Chapter 3 Lessons 1–5

Review: Synonyms and Antonyms, Analogies

Read each word pair. Write **A** on the line if the words are antonyms and write **S** on the line if the words are synonyms.

1. _____ negotiating   bargaining
2. _____ elderly   aged
3. _____ excitable   easy-going
4. _____ curtains   drapery
5. _____ puzzling   clear
6. _____ confident   assured
7. _____ revealed   concealed
8. _____ disturbed   avoided
9. _____ original   unique
10. _____ agreeable   argumentative

11. _____ anxious   jittery
12. _____ arch   curve
13. _____ segment   whole
14. _____ guard   protector
15. _____ enthusiastic   reluctant
16. _____ honest   candid
17. _____ shanty   mansion
18. _____ secretary   assistant
19. _____ praise   ridicule
20. _____ fence   enclosure

Circle the word in parentheses that best completes each analogy.

1. glass : (cup, plate) : : horse : pony
2. gift : wrapping paper : : baby : (rattle, blanket)
3. lamp : (electricity, light) : : hose : water
4. meter : yard : : kilogram : (pound, scale)
5. (the moon, the sun) : Earth : : Jupiter : the sun
6. carving : wood : : (cutting, drawing) : paper
7. solid : liquid : : fall : (plummet, rise)
8. book : library : : (horse, farm) : barn
9. waiter : (restaurant, cook) : : judge : courthouse
10. pinecone : needle : : (acorn, branch) : leaf
11. summer : (beach, swimming) : : winter : skiing
12. deer : herd : : fish : (bunch, school)

Lesson 3.6 Homophones

Homophones are words that sound the same but have different spellings and different meanings. There are hundreds of homophones in the English language.

     raised—lifted
     razed—tore down

     real—actual and true
     reel—a cylinder on which material can be wound

     gored—pierced or stabbed
     gourd—hard-shelled fruit

If you are unsure about which homophone to use, look up the meanings in a dictionary.

Identify It

Circle the correct homophone(s) in each sentence.

1. The child (balled, bald, bawled) when her ice cream cone fell to the ground.

2. When Ms. Chan announced the pop quiz, the class let out a (groan, grown).

3. The (yews, ewes, use) growing alongside our house have gotten much (to, too, two) big.

4. When the (tide, tied) goes out, the dock rests on the ground.

5. "The chalice is made of solid 24-(carrot, karat, caret) gold," the guide explained.

6. Sofia (lead, led) her friends to the backyard (wear, where) she (lets, let's) her kitten play.

7. Mom (told, tolled) me she was not (aloud, allowed) to wear (jeans, genes) until she was an adult.

8. The Joneses had a skylight installed in the (sealing, ceiling) of (their, they're, there) living room.

9. Mr. Brown's science class is studying (cells, sells) this semester.

10. Tow trucks arrived at the (seen, scene) of the accident.

11. On the last page of (your, you're) report, be sure to (sight, site, cite) the sources you used.

12. Crosby is (do, dew, due) for a checkup.

13. The (soles, souls) of Candace's (shoos, shoes) are quite (worn, warn).

14. Next (week, weak) the school is (reseeding, receding) the (bare, bear) spots on the soccer field.

Lesson 3.6 Homophones

Proof It
Proofread the following dialogue. It contains multiple errors in homophones. There are 26 mistakes to correct in all.

> *e* – deletes incorrect letters, words, punctuation
> ^ – inserts correct letters, words, punctuation

"Hay, Dad," exclaimed Russ, "I've decided what I want to bee when I'm dun with school."

"That's good gnus," said Dad. "Halve a seat and tell me awl about it wile you eat you're serial."

"I want too work with dinosaurs," explained Russ. "Well, at leased what is left of them. I want to be a paleontologist."

"Don't paleontologists study moor than just dinosaurs? I think they also study ancient plants and microorganisms. You knead to have your science teacher council you on the different areas you could pursue," suggested Dad.

"That's exactly what I plan to dew," piped inn Russ. "I'm going to meat with the school guidance counselor and discuss the classes I should sine up for next. I also herd theirs a paleontologist giving a tock at the museum next weak."

"I think you have set a nice coarse for yourself," continued Dad. "Now, I'm late for the city counsel meeting. Isle sea you later."

Try It
Choose six of the misused homophones that appear in the paragraph above. Write a sentence for each word using the correct meaning.

1. _____

2. _____

3. _____

4. _____

5. _____

6. _____

Lesson 3.7 Multiple-Meaning Words

Multiple-meaning words, or **homographs**, are words that are spelled the same but have different meanings. They may also sometimes have different pronunciations.

The word *sow* can mean "to plant seeds" or it can mean "a female pig."
Before you *sow* the seeds, be sure the soil is moist.
Twelve piglets trotted along behind the *sow*.

Rewrite It

Read each sentence below. Then, write a new sentence using a different meaning for the underlined word. Use a dictionary if you need help.

1. The photographs look best if you let the <u>monitor</u> warm up for an hour or so.

_____

2. Be careful when you <u>season</u> the chili; we don't want it to be too spicy.

_____

3. Mr. McMasters will <u>prune</u> the crabapple trees on Saturday.

_____

4. We are having <u>company</u> stay with us over Labor Day weekend.

_____

5. In the summer, Aunt Flo loves to add a sprig of <u>mint</u> to her iced tea.

_____

6. The stain on Hanna's shirt is so <u>minute</u>, no one will notice.

_____

7. Dr. Lucas measured the electrical <u>current</u> running through the wire.

_____

8. The bridge's steel beams were designed not to <u>buckle</u> under the weight of traffic.

_____

9. Kyle's mother is a talented <u>sewer</u> and made all the costumes for the play.

_____

10. We had to buy a <u>permit</u> in order to sell shirts at the concert.

_____

11. Ms. Walker attended the council meeting to <u>contest</u> the new budget.

_____

Lesson 3.7 Multiple-Meaning Words

Solve It

Read each pair of definitions below the word search. Think of the multiple-meaning word that fits both definitions and then find it in the word search puzzle. Words may be written horizontally or vertically, backward or forward.

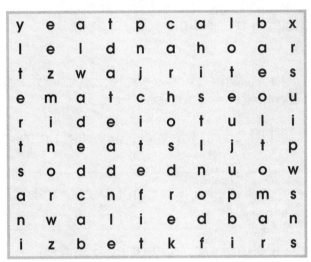

1. younger than 18 years old; less important

    _____ _____ _____ _____ _____

2. category or type; friendly and generous

    _____ _____ _____ _____

3. guide or control; bull raised for beef

    _____ _____ _____ _____ _____

4. see romantically; specific day of the month or year

    _____ _____ _____ _____

5. part used for carrying or holding; manage or manipulate

    _____ _____ _____ _____ _____ _____

6. pillar supporting a roof or ceiling; regular section of a newspaper or magazine

    _____ _____ _____ _____ _____ _____

7. injury; past tense of *wind*

    _____ _____ _____ _____ _____

8. piece of wood or paper used to start a fire; contest

    _____ _____ _____ _____ _____

Lesson 3.8 Connotations and Denotations

A word's **denotation** is its actual, literal meaning. It is the meaning you would find if you looked the word up in a dictionary.

A word's **connotation** is the meaning associated with the word. The connotation may be more emotional, or tied to an idea or feeling about the word. Connotations can be positive, negative, or neutral.

For example, the words *skinny, scrawny, slender,* and *slim* all mean approximately the same thing. Their denotation is "not weighing very much; not overweight." The connotation of these words, however, is different. *Scrawny* has a negative connotation—it brings to mind a person or animal that is unhealthy and underweight. *Slender* and *slim* both have a positive connotation—they sound attractive and healthy. *Skinny* can have a positive, negative, or neutral connotation, depending on how it is used.

Identify It
Read each phrase below. On the line, write *positive, negative,* or *neutral,* depending on the connotation of the *italicized* word.

1. a strong *aroma* _____

a strong *odor* _____

a strong *fragrance* _____

a strong *scent* _____

2. a *sloppy* outfit _____

a *casual* outfit _____

3. the *fragile* display _____

the *flimsy* display _____

4. a *cheap* dinner _____

an *inexpensive* dinner _____

a *frugal* dinner _____

5. the *colorful* scarf _____

the *gaudy* scarf _____

the *vivid* scarf _____

6. a *fussy* student _____

a *conscientious* student _____

a *meticulous* student _____

Lesson 3.8 Connotations and Denotations

Complete It

Complete each sentence below with a word from the box. The word you choose should have a similar denotation but different connotation from the word in parentheses.

skittish	squandered	lost	pushy
calculated	fussy	glower	exceptional

1. Many people think that Leah has an (odd) _____ sense of humor.

2. Thomas (spent) _____ his allowance on graphic novels.

3. If you ask her opinion, Jordan will give you a (thoughtful) _____ response.

4. Don't worry about your stuffed bear, Ananya—I'm sure we just (misplaced) _____ it.

5. The design of the handbags is quite (detailed) _____.

6. Please try not to (stare) _____ at the toddler having a temper tantrum.

7. Although my cousin appears (timid) _____ when you first meet her, she's actually very friendly.

8. If you are (confident) _____ in your beliefs, others will respect your viewpoint.

Try It

Write a sentence for each word below. The words in each pair have similar denotations but different connotations.

1. nosy _____

   inquisitive _____

2. unique _____

   bizarre _____

3. hoard _____

   collect _____

4. energetic _____

   wild _____

Lesson 3.9 Figures of Speech: Similes, Metaphors, and Personification

A **simile** is a figure of speech that compares two things using the words *like* or *as*.
> *The children slept snuggled like puppies* on the pile of blankets.
> *The tiny charm* on Ella's necklace was *as delicate and perfect as a snowflake.*

A **metaphor** is a figure of speech that compares two unlike things that are similar in some way.
> *The runner's steps were a metronome,* thumping a steady beat along the street.
> *The setting sun was a ball of fire* in the dusky sky.

Personification is a figure of speech that gives human characteristics to something that is not human.
> *The raindrops ran merrily* down the window panes.
> *The cardinal boastfully declared* that he had found the prettiest mate in all the town.

Identify It

Read each example of figurative language. On the line, tell what two things are being compared and what figure of speech is used (simile, metaphor, or personification).

1. On the last day of school before summer vacation, Ms. Lottig's class was a zoo.

_____

2. Gloria's hurtful words shot like bullets across the room.

_____

3. Alexander knows that an education is the key to his future, which is why he works so hard at school.

_____

4. Nico looked like a sheepdog, peering out from underneath his shaggy bangs.

_____

5. The wrinkles on Grandma's face were a roadmap to the places her life had taken her.

_____

6. Silence hung over the room like a heavy veil.

_____

7. The last tree stood in the empty lot, a soldier awaiting orders.

_____

Lesson 3.9 Figures of Speech: Similes, Metaphors, and Personification

Rewrite It

Rewrite each sentence below using a simile, metaphor, or personification to make the writing more descriptive or interesting to read. Make sure to use each type of figure of speech at least once.

1. The icicles hung from the edge of the porch roof.

_____

2. The sun streamed in the windows.

_____

3. The children ran screaming into the playground.

_____

4. Hail bounced against the tin roof for hours.

_____

5. Grace's new moped was shiny and red.

_____

6. The laundry on the line blew in the gentle breeze.

_____

7. Grandpa Charles was a large man who often wore a stern expression.

_____

8. The subway car rumbled into the station.

_____

9. As the deer walked through the woods, leaves crackled underfoot.

_____

10. The flames grew larger as the curtains caught on fire.

_____

Lesson 3.9 Figures of Speech: Similes, Metaphors, and Personification

Identify It
Underline the ten figures of speech in the following selection.

On Tuesday afternoon, Alejandra and her aunt Sofia packed the trunk of the car and set off on their camping trip. As they eased out of the driveway, the tired old station wagon heaved in protest, but Sofia just grinned and waved good-bye to Alejandra's parents.

"This is going to be so much fun!" exclaimed Alejandra. "I've been looking forward to this trip for ages."

"Me, too," agreed Sofia. "Work has been so stressful lately. But as soon as we got on the road, I felt as free as a bird let out of its cage."

Two hours later, Alejandra and Sofia pulled into the campground and began setting up the tent. "Grrr!" said Sofia, as she struggled with the poles. "This tent is like a puzzle that is missing half the pieces."

Her niece laughed. "No it's not, Aunt Sofia, you're just terrible at following instructions." Alejandra took the crumpled page from her aunt, and in minutes, the dark blue tent stood proudly at attention, happy to welcome them inside.

After a dinner of grilled chicken and corn on the cob, Alejandra and Sofia built a campfire as it began to get dark. The fire cracked and hissed like meat sizzling in a hot pan, and sparks danced and twirled gracefully into the sky.

"Look at that," remarked Sofia, gesturing to the dark blue sky. "The sky is an empty canvas. I'm going to sit right here and watch it fill up with stars." She pulled the woolly blanket around herself until she was wrapped as tightly as a burrito. "That's cozy," she said sleepily. "I could stay here all night."

"I know," said Alejandra, "but I hear my pillow calling for me. I don't think I'll last much longer." She tossed a twig into the fire and stood up, stretching her back. A small movement caught Alejandra's eye, and she peered around the side of the tent. A fat raccoon with eyes gleaming like headlights munched on a discarded corn cob. Alejandra laughed. "Looks like we're not the only ones who enjoy corn for dinner!"

Try It
Describe a place that makes you feel calm and peaceful. Use at least three similes and/or metaphors in your description.

_____

_____

_____

_____

Lesson 3.9 Figures of Speech: Similes, Metaphors, and Personification

Complete It
Complete each simile below with a word from the box.

hills	wind	gold	baby
feather	mule	bone	honey

1. as sweet as _____

2. runs like the _____

3. slept like a _____

4. as stubborn as a _____

5. as old as the _____

6. as good as _____

7. as light as a _____

8. as dry as a _____

Try It
On the lines below, write comparisons based on the instructions.

1. Write a metaphor related to music.

_____

2. Write a simile that includes something related to cooking.

_____

3. Write a sentence personifying a natural event.

_____

4. Write a metaphor about a type of vehicle.

_____

5. Write a simile that includes some type of weather.

_____

6. Write a sentence personifying a wild animal.

_____

7. Write a metaphor about a season.

_____

Review   Chapter 3 Lessons 6–9

Review: Homophones, Multiple-Meaning Words

Read each definition. Choose the correct homophone from the box and write it on the line beside the definition.

dense	stationary	serial	stationery	dents
symbol	muscle	cymbal	mussel	cereal

1. _____ describes the numbers on a piece of money

2. _____ breakfast food eaten with milk

3. _____ something that represents something else

4. _____ a percussion instrument made of two metal plates that are clapped together

5. _____ thick; crowded together

6. _____ marks or indentations

7. _____ standing still; unmoving

8. _____ writing paper or materials

9. _____ a bivalve sea creature, similar to a clam

10. _____ an organ in the body that produces movement

Read each sentence. Then, circle the letter of the definition that describes the meaning of the underlined word as it is used in the sentence.

1. Bryan caught an enormous <u>bass</u> last weekend.

   a. a deep sound   **b.** a type of fish

2. The lamp has a manufacturing <u>defect</u>, so I plan to return it.

   a. a flaw or imperfection   **b.** to desert a country

3. Mischa's grandmother has been an <u>invalid</u> for several years.

   a. a weak, sickly person   **b.** not valid, sound, or just

4. Serena Williams was declared the winner of the tennis <u>match</u>.

   a. a thin piece of wood used for starting a fire   **b.** a game or contest of skills

5. What's your favorite school <u>subject</u> this year?

   a. to expose to something   **b.** topic of study

Review Chapter 3 Lessons 6–9

Review: Connotations and Denotations, Figures of Speech

Write a sentence using each boldface word below. Follow the sentence by adding whether the word, as you used it, has a positive, neutral, or negative connotation.

1. unusual _____

_____

2. unique _____

_____

3. bizarre _____

_____

4. ambitious _____

_____

5. greedy _____

_____

6. confident _____

_____

7. arrogant _____

_____

Each sentence below contains a simile, a metaphor, or personification. Underline each figure of speech, and write **S**, **M**, or **P** on the line to tell what type of figure of speech it is.

1. Steam rose out of Yumi's hot cocoa, leaving a trail behind like a tiny airplane. _____

2. The crispy bagel eagerly jumped out of the toaster and waited patiently on the counter for Mr. Olivieri to pick her up. _____

3. Mr. Rozek's stern gaze was a spotlight, making Noah feel uncomfortable and nervous. _____

4. The kite swooped, ducked, and darted through the air like an excited chickadee. _____

5. The sunlight was a puddle of gold on the floor of Mei-Ling's bedroom. _____

6. The scent of hot pancakes and maple bacon beckoned enticingly to Damon from the kitchen. _____

Lesson 4.1 Writer's Guide: Prewriting

The five steps of the writing process are **prewriting**, **drafting**, **revising**, **proofreading**, and **publishing**.

Prewriting, the first stage of the writing process, involves planning and organizing. This is the stage where you get the ideas for your paper and start plotting it out.

When you prewrite, you:

- Think of ideas for your topic that are not too narrow or too broad. Write down your chosen ideas.

- Select your favorite topic, the one you think you can write about the best.

- Write down anything that comes to your mind about your chosen topic. Don't worry about grammar and spelling at this stage. This is called *freewriting*.

- Organize your information the way you might organize it in your paper. Use a graphic organizer. Graphic organizers visually represent the layout and ideas for a written paper. Graphic organizers include spider maps, Venn diagrams, story boards, network trees, and outlines.

- Use your graphic organizer to find out what information you already know and what information you need to learn more about.

Prewriting Example

Assignment: biography of a hero

Topic ideas: Martin Luther King, Jr., Eleanor Roosevelt, Jesse Owens, Cleveland Amory, Lance Armstrong, Rachel Carson

Freewriting of selected topic: Cleveland Amory hero of animals. Author. Founder of the Fund for Animals. Wrote The Cat Who Came for Christmas. Read Black Beauty as a child and wanted a ranch for rescued animals. Established Black Beauty Ranch for rescued animals.

Graphic organizer:

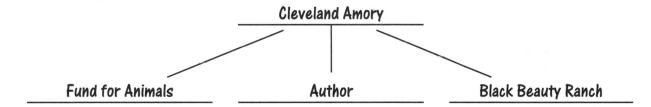

Cleveland Amory

Fund for Animals   Author   Black Beauty Ranch

Lesson 4.2 Writer's Guide: Drafting

Drafting involves writing your rough draft. Don't worry too much about grammar and spelling. Write down all of your thoughts about the subject, based on the structure of your graphic organizer.

When you draft, you:

- Write an **introduction** with a topic sentence. Get your readers' attention by stating a startling statistic or asking a question. Explain the purpose of your writing.

- Write the **body** of your paper. Use your graphic organizer to decide how many paragraphs will be included in your paper. Write one paragraph for each idea.

- Write your **conclusion**. Your conclusion will summarize your paper.

Drafting Example

My hero was a hero: a hero to animals. Cleveland Amory (1917–1998) was an author, an animal advocate, and an animal rescuer. Reading <u>Black Beauty</u> as a child inspired a dream for Amory. Cleveland Amory made his dream a reality.

Amory founded The Fund for Animals. The Fund for Animals is an animal advocacy group that campaigns for animal protection. Amory served as its president, without pay, until his death in 1998. Cleveland Amory was an editor. He was an editor for <u>The Saturday Evening Post</u>. He served in World War II. After world war II, he wrote history books that studied society. He was a commentator on The Today Show, a critic for <u>TV guide</u>, a columnist for <u>Saturday Review</u>. Amory especially loved his own cat, Polar Bear, who inspired him to write three instant best-selling books: <u>The Cat Who Came for Christmas</u>, <u>The Cat and the Curmudgeon</u>, and <u>The Best Cat Ever</u>.

When Amory read <u>Black Beauty</u> as a child. When he read <u>Black Beauty</u>, he dreamed of place where animals could roam free and live in caring conditions. The dream is real at Black Beauty Ranch, a sanctuary for abused and abandoned animals The ranch's 1,620 acres serve as home for hundreds of animals, including elephants, horses, burros, ostriches, chimpanzees, and many more. Black Beauty Ranch takes in unwanted, abused, neglected, abandoned, and rescued domestic and exotic animals.

Cleveland Amory is my hero because he is a hero. He worked to make his dreams realities. His best-selling books, the founding of The Fund for Animals, and the opening of Black Beauty Ranch are the legacy of his dreams. Words from Anna Sewell's <u>Black Beauty</u>, the words that inspired Cleveland Amory, are engraved at the entrance to Black Beauty Ranch: "I have nothing to fear; and here my story ends. My troubles are all over, and I am at home." Cleveland Amory died on October 15, 1998. He is buried at Black Beauty Ranch, next to his beloved cat, Polar Bear.

Lesson 4.3 Writer's Guide: Revising

Revising is the time to stop and think about what you have already written. It is time to rewrite.

When you revise, you:

- Add or change words.
- Delete unnecessary words or phrases.
- Move text around.
- Improve the overall flow of your paper.

Revising Example (body of paper)

Cleveland Amory did more than just write about the animals he loved.
                              in 1967   one of the world's most active
  ^Amory founded The Fund for Animals. The Fund for Animals is an animal advocacy
                     rights and
group that campaigns for animal protection. Amory served as its president, without
                Amory extended his devotion to animals with Black Beauty Ranch.
                                 started his writing career as
pay, until his death in 1998. Cleveland Amory was an editor. He was an editor for The
                                                 serving in
Saturday Evening Post. ~~He served in World War II.~~ After world war II, he wrote history

books that studied society. He was a commentator on The Today Show, a critic for TV
                    Amory's love of animals, as well as great affection for
guide, a columnist for Saturday Review. ~~Amory especially loved~~ his own cat, Polar Bear,
             led
~~who inspired~~ him to ~~write~~ three instant best-selling books: The Cat Who Came for

Christmas, The Cat and the Curmudgeon, and The Best Cat Ever.

     Cleveland Amory made his childhood dream come true in 1979 when he
          opened Black Beauty Ranch in Texas.
     ~~When Amory read Black Beauty as a child.~~ When he read Black Beauty, he

dreamed of place where animals could roam free and live in caring conditions. The
          for hundreds of
dream is real at Black Beauty Ranch, ~~a sanctuary for abused and abandoned animals~~

The ranch's 1,620 acres serve as home for ~~hundreds of animals, including~~ elephants,
                                                      animals
horses, burros, ostriches, chimpanzees, and many more. ~~Black Beauty Ranch takes in~~

unwanted, abused, neglected, abandoned, and rescued domestic and exotic

animals.

Lesson 4.4 Writer's Guide: Proofreading

Proofreading is the time to look for more technical errors.

When you proofread, you:

- Check spelling.
- Check grammar.
- Check punctuation.

Proofreading Example (body of paper after revision)

Cleveland Amory started his writing career as an editor for <u>The Saturday Evening</u> <u>Post</u>. After serving in World War II, he wrote history books that studied society. He was a commentator on <u>The Today Show</u>, a critic for <u>TV guide</u>, a columnist for <u>Saturday</u> <u>Review</u>. Amory's love of animals, as well as great affection for his own cat, Polar Bear, led him to three instant best-selling books: <u>The Cat Who Came for Christmas</u>, <u>The Cat</u> <u>and the Curmudgeon</u>, and <u>The Best Cat Ever</u>.

Cleveland Amory did more than just write about the animals he loved. Amory founded The Fund for Animals in 1967. The Fund for Animals is one of the world's most active animal advocacy group that campaigns for animal rights and protection. Amory served as its president, without pay, until his death in 1998. Amory extended his devotion to animals with Black Beauty Ranch.

Cleveland Amory made his childhood dream come true in 1979 when he opened Black Beauty Ranch in Texas. He dreamed of place where animals could roam free and live in caring conditions. The dream is real for hundreds of unwanted, abused, neglected, abandoned, and rescued domestic and exotic animals at Black Beauty Ranch. The ranch's 1,620 acres serve as home for elephants, horses, burros, ostriches, chimpanzees, and many more animals.

Lesson 4.5 Writer's Guide: Publishing

Publishing is the fifth and final stage of the writing process. Write your final copy and decide how you want to publish your work. Here is a list of some ideas:

- Read your paper to family and classmates.

- Illustrate and hang class papers in a "Hall of Fame" in your class or school.

- Publish your work in a school or community newspaper or magazine.

Publishing (compare to the other three versions to see how it has improved)

Biography of a Hero: Cleveland Amory

My hero was a hero: a hero to animals. Cleveland Amory (1917–1998) was an author, an animal advocate, and an animal rescuer. Reading Black Beauty as a child inspired a dream for Amory. Cleveland Amory made his dream a reality.

Cleveland Amory started his writing career as an editor for The Saturday Evening Post. After serving in World War II, Amory wrote history books that studied society. He was a commentator on The Today Show, a critic for TV Guide, and a columnist for Saturday Review. Amory's love of animals, as well as great affection for his own cat Polar Bear, led him to three instant best-selling books: The Cat Who Came for Christmas, The Cat and the Curmudgeon, and The Best Cat Ever.

Cleveland Amory did more than just write about the animals he loved. Amory founded The Fund for Animals in 1967. The Fund for Animals is one of the world's most active animal advocacy groups that campaigns for animal rights and protection. Amory served as its president, without pay, until his death in 1998. Amory extended his devotion to animals with Black Beauty Ranch.

Cleveland Amory made his childhood dream come true in 1979 when he opened Black Beauty Ranch in Texas. He dreamed of a place where animals could roam free and live in caring conditions. The dream is real for hundreds of unwanted, abused, neglected, abandoned, and rescued domestic and exotic animals at Black Beauty Ranch. The ranch's 1,620 acres serve as home for elephants, horses, burros, ostriches, chimpanzees, and many more animals.

Cleveland Amory is my hero because he is a hero. He worked to make his dreams realities. His best-selling books, the founding of The Fund for Animals, and the opening of Black Beauty Ranch are the legacy of his dreams. Words from Anna Sewell's Black Beauty, the words that inspired Cleveland Amory, are engraved at the entrance to Black Beauty Ranch: "I have nothing to fear; and here my story ends. My troubles are all over, and I am at home." Cleveland Amory died on October 15, 1998. He is buried at Black Beauty Ranch, next to his beloved cat, Polar Bear.

Lesson 4.6 Writer's Guide: Evaluating Writing

When you are evaluating your own writing and the writing of others, being a critic is a good thing.

You can learn a lot about how you write by reading and rereading papers you have written. As you continue to write, your techniques will improve. You can look at previous papers and evaluate them. How would you change them to improve them knowing what you know now?

You can also look at the writing of others: classmates, school reporters, newspaper and magazine writers, and authors. Evaluate their writing, too. You can learn about different styles from reading a variety of written works. Be critical with their writing. How would you improve it?

Take the points covered in the Writer's Guide and make a checklist. You can use this checklist to evaluate your writing and others' writing, too. Add other items to the checklist as you come across them or think of them.

Evaluation Checklist

❏ Write an introduction with a topic sentence that will get your readers' attention. Explain the purpose of your writing.

❏ Write the body with one paragraph for each idea.

❏ Write a conclusion that summarizes the paper, stating the main points.

❏ Add or change words.

❏ Delete unnecessary words or phrases.

❏ Move text around.

❏ Improve the overall flow of your paper.

❏ Check spelling.

❏ Check grammar.

❏ Check punctuation.

❏ _____

❏ _____

❏ _____

Lesson 4.7 Writer's Guide: Writing Process Practice

The following pages may be used to practice the writing process.

Prewriting

Assignment: _____

_____

Topic ideas: _____

_____

_____

Freewriting of selected topic: _____

_____

_____

_____

_____

_____

_____

_____

_____

_____

_____

_____

Graphic Organizer:

Lesson 4.7 | Writer's Guide: Writing Process Practice

Drafting

_____

_____

_____

_____

_____

_____

_____

_____

_____

_____

_____

_____

_____

_____

_____

_____

_____

_____

_____

_____

_____

_____

_____

_____

_____

_____

_____

Lesson 4.7 Writer's Guide: Writing Process Practice

Revising

_____

_____

_____

_____

_____

_____

_____

_____

_____

_____

_____

_____

_____

_____

_____

_____

_____

_____

_____

_____

_____

_____

_____

_____

_____

_____

_____

_____

_____

Lesson 4.7 Writer's Guide: Writing Process Practice

Proofreading

_____

_____

_____

_____

_____

_____

_____

_____

_____

_____

_____

_____

_____

_____

_____

_____

_____

_____

_____

_____

_____

_____

_____

_____

_____

_____

_____

_____

_____

Lesson 4.7   Writer's Guide: Writing Process Practice

Publishing

Final Draft: Include illustrations, photographs, graphic aids, etc.

_____

_____

_____

_____

_____

_____

_____

_____

_____

_____

_____

_____

_____

_____

_____

_____

_____

_____

_____

_____

_____

_____

_____

_____

_____

_____

_____

_____

_____

Common nouns name people, places, things, and ideas.

    People: butcher, nephew, landscaper, jogger, teenager, pilot
    Places: home, ice cream shop, college, bookstore, basement
    Things: violet, floor, photograph, pond, mercury, government
    Ideas: happiness, freedom, anxiety, enthusiasm, truth

Proper nouns name specific people, places, and things. Proper nouns are capitalized.

    People: Charlie, Mr. Rodriguez, Dr. Chang, Officer Bates
    Places: Tijuana, Yellowstone National Park, Virginia
    Things: Tasty Time Pizza, the Iron Age

Identify It
Underline the common noun(s) and circle the proper noun(s) in each sentence.

1. Most people consider the (Home Insurance Building) to be the first skyscraper.
2. It was built in (Chicago) in 1884 and rose to a height of ten stories.
3. Others think the (Jayne Building) in (Philadelphia) should have the honor.
4. For nearly 40 years, the (Empire State Building) in (New York City) was the tallest building on (Earth).
5. The (World Trade Center) held the record for two years, but then the (Sears Tower) was completed.
6. The (Sears Tower) known today as (Willis Tower) was overtaken by the (Petronas Towers) in (Kuala Lumpur) the capital of (Malaysia).
7. (Taipei 101) in (Taiwan) was the first building to exceed 500 meters in height.
8. The tallest skyscraper in the world is the (Burj Khalifa) in the city of (Dubai).

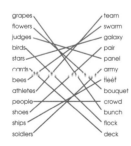

5

Proof It
Correct the mistakes in the use of common and proper nouns using proofreading marks.

/ – lowercase letter
≡ – capitalize letter

1. We are going to visit grandpa Mick in Tampa bay, Florida, next Week.
2. My Brother Tim plans to bring along his fishing pole and tackle box.
3. He and Grandpa will drive to lake Harris on monday to catch Trout and Catfish.
4. On Tuesday, my Mom and Dad are riding their Mountain Bikes on wilkin's swamp trail.
5. I'm looking forward to Wednesday Afternoon, when we will be heading to ronnie's reptile world to see the alligators.
6. My grandpa loves listening to old frank sinatra records while he dances around the Living Room.
7. As soon as we get home, I have to finish writing my Report about the declaration of independence.
8. Mr. Woodlock is my History Teacher at Broughten jr. high school.

Try It
Write a paragraph about your favorite book or movie. Use at least six common and six proper nouns correctly.

_____

_____

Answers will vary.

_____

_____

6

Collective nouns are used to describe groups of specific animals, people, or things.

    A group of horses is a *herd*.
    A group of students is a *class*.
    A group of mountains is a *range*.

A collective noun refers to more than one thing, but it acts as a singular noun when used in a sentence.

    Incorrect: The *herd are* running back to the barn.
    Correct: The *herd is* running back to the barn.

Abstract nouns describe ideas rather than people, places, or things that can be perceived with the five senses.

    courage   laziness   information   beauty   hate

Match It
Match each plural noun in the left column with its singular collective noun in the right column.

grapes	team
flowers	swarm
judges	galaxy
birds	pair
stars	panel
cards	army
bees	fleet
athletes	bouquet
people	crowd
shoes	bunch
ships	flock
soldiers	deck

7

Complete It
Circle the verb in each sentence that correctly completes the sentence.

1. The staff (is are) getting the day off work because of a holiday.
2. A pride of lions (stalk, (stalks)) the savannah in search of food.
3. Courageousness (mean, (means)) feeling scared but taking action anyway.
4. The entire neighborhood (attend, (attends)) the annual block party.
5. The dance troupe (perform, (performs)) three shows each Saturday this month.
6. The crew (prepare, (prepares)) the ship for its long journey to the South Seas.
7. A choir (sing, (sings)) at the mall during the Christmas season.
8. The fleet (sail, (sails)) from San Francisco to Honolulu and back again each spring.
9. My family (is are) volunteering at the food pantry this weekend.
10. Beth's singing ability (enable, (enables)) her to join any chorus she chooses.
11. The audience (cheer, (cheers)) as the magician grabs a scarf out of a puff of smoke.
12. A team of horses (pull, (pulls)) the wagon across a desolate, frozen prairie.

Try It
For ~~each~~ ... ~~sentence~~ that uses it correctly. If you are unsure of a nou~~n~~ ... find its definition.

Answers may vary.
Possible answers :

| success | justice | misery | anger | parenthood |
| leisure | compassion | friendship | loyalty | curiosity |

Success depends on hard work.
Leisure is something I seldom enjoy.
The lawyer fought for justice.
My compassion for animals is well known.
The misery he felt brought tears to his eyes.
Our friendship has lasted for decades.
Do not speak in anger.
His loyalty to the company knows no limits.
They never had the chance to experience the joys of parenthood.
My curiosity led me to the library.

8

Panel 9:

Although **plural** and **possessive nouns** often sound similar, they are spelled differently and have different meanings.
  Plural noun: The *bats* roost deep within the cave.
  Singular possessive noun: The *bat's* roost is located deep within the cave.
  Plural possessive noun: The *bats'* roost is located deep within the cave.

Rewrite It
Rewrite each sentence to correct the word in bold.

1. **Cave's** are not the only places where bats roost.
   Caves are not the only places where bats roost.

2. These flying **mammals** homes are also found beneath bridges and inside hollow trees.
   These flying mammals' homes are also found beneath bridges and inside hollow trees.

3. **Predators'** don't think to look for bats in these out-of-the-way places.
   Predators don't think to look for bats in these out-of-the-way places.

4. Bats cluster together in **colony's** because it keeps them warm and safe.
   Bats cluster together in colonies because it keeps them warm and safe.

5. Unlike birds, **bats** wings are not strong enough to lift them from the ground and into the air.
   Unlike birds, bats' wings are not strong enough to lift them from the ground and into the air.

6. A **bats'** hind legs are also weak, so they cannot get a running start.
   A bat's hind legs are also weak, so they cannot get a running start.

7. Instead, bats use their **claws'** to climb to a high place.
   Instead, bats use their claws to climb to a high place.

8. The **claw's** grip the surface, and the bat relaxes.
   The claws grip the surface, and the bat relaxes.

9. **Gravities** pull locks the claws—and the bat—in place.
   Gravity's pull locks the claws--and the bat--in place.

10. The **bats'** muscles do not need to exert any energy.
    The bat's muscles do not need to exert any energy.

9

Panel 10:

Identify It
Look at the boldface word in each sentence. On the line, write **PL** if the word is a plural noun, **SP** if the word is a singular possessive, and **PP** if the word is a plural possessive.

1. _PL_ The **paleontologists** flew to Montana to hunt for fossils.
2. _SP_ **Dr. Harris's** plane touched down on a grassy runway in the middle of nowhere.
3. _PP_ As the plane bounced along, the **scientists'** equipment rattled around inside steel boxes.
4. _PL_ The steep, rocky **sides** of a mountain towered over the flat valley.
5. _SP_ A local **rancher's** pickup waited near the runway.
6. _PL_ The truck would carry the **boxes** of equipment to the dig site.
7. _SP_ Dr. Gupta drove the truck across the **valley's** bumpy landscape.
8. _PP_ **Clouds'** shadows moved slowly over the distant mountain.
9. _SP_ An hour later, the scientists arrived at the **mountain's** base.
10. _PL_ A camp had been set up, with several **tents** encircling a large fire pit.
11. _SP_ The excavation **site's** location was within walking distance of the camp.
12. _PP_ The **doctors'** excitement was easy to see; they both had huge grins on their faces!

Try It
Write ~~the~~ [Answers may vary.] of the words below. ~~Use~~ [Possible answers :] ~~right~~ word.

| dinosaurs | dinosaur's | dinosaurs' |

1. Dinosaurs exist today only as fossils.

2. The dinosaur's diet consisted of only vegetation.

3. Dinosaurs' teeth have been found around the world.

10

Panel 11:

An **appositive** is a noun or phrase that renames another noun in a sentence. The appositive offers more information about the noun.

  Harriet, *a golden retriever*, has been my constant companion since she was a puppy.
  The phrase *a golden retriever* is an appositive that renames *Harriet*.

When the appositive is non-essential, or not necessary to the sentence, it should have a comma before and after it. In the example above, you can remove the appositive and the sentence still makes sense.

Identify It
Read each sentence below. Underline the appositives. Circle the nouns they rename.

1. The (Windsor Pumpkin Regatta), a water race in Nova Scotia, was begun in 1999.
2. (Danny Dill), the founder of the race, is the son of a breeder of giant pumpkins.
3. (Contestants), who must paddle half a mile, use giant hollowed-out pumpkins as small watercraft.
4. (The regatta), the first of its kind, has inspired other races around North America.
5. The first step in creating pumpkin boats is to hollow out (giant pumpkins), some of which weigh 700 pounds!
6. The (pumpkin), which rots relatively quickly, needs to be hollowed up just a day or two before the race.
7. A (pumpkin boat), also known as a personal vegetable craft (PVC), is not easy to navigate.
8. (Leo Swinamer), a nine-time winner of the regatta, is in his mid-seventies!
9. The (race), which has three classes, is attended by thousands of spectators every year.
10. The first person to use a pumpkin as a boat was (Wayne Hackney), a pumpkin farmer from New Hampshire.

11

Panel 12:

Proof It
Read the paragraph below. It contains five appositives that are missing commas. Use this proofreading symbol ‸ to add commas where they are needed.

Pumpkins‸ a type of squash‸ are a symbol of fall to many people. These large ribbed fruits are round in shape, heavy, and filled with seeds. Pumpkin vines‸ which wind their way through pumpkin patches‸ can be covered in small prickly hairs. This can make picking a little irritating! In recent years, pick-your-own pumpkin patches have increased in popularity. Many families enjoy the tradition of a yearly trip to the patch. Pumpkins‸ which are often carved at Halloween‸ also have many other uses. Many people like to eat pumpkin pie‸ a tradition at Thanksgiving. Pumpkin muffins, bread, and cheesecake also have their fans. Although most people use pureed pumpkin, the flowers, seeds, and leaves are also edible. The seeds‸ a delicious snack when roasted‸ can be a healthy, nutritious treat.

Try It
Write four sentences on the lines below. Each one should contain an appositive. Remember to punctuate the appositives correctly.

1. _____

2. _____ [Answers will vary.]

3. _____

4. _____

12

Page 13

A **pronoun** is a word used in place of a noun. A **subject pronoun** can be used as the subject of a sentence. It can be singular (*I, you, he, she, it*) or plural (*we, you, they*).

She hoped that Uncle Ralph would visit on Sunday.

An **object pronoun** is the object of a verb or a preposition. It can also be singular (*me, you, him, her, it*) or plural (*us, you, them*).

Clare wanted *us* to go to the concert tomorrow night.

A **possessive pronoun** shows possession. Singular possessive pronouns are *my, mine, your, yours, his, her, hers,* and *its,* and plural possessive pronouns are *our, ours, your, yours, their,* and *theirs.*

Their sprinkler has been on for three hours.

Identify It
Read each sentence below and decide how the **boldface** pronoun is used. On the line, write **SP** for subject pronoun, **OP** for object pronoun, or **PP** for possessive pronoun.

1. **PP** Kembe and **his** dad like to explore caves together.
2. **SP** **They** first started spelunking, or caving, when Kembe was twelve.
3. **OP** Kembe's parents gave **him** some gear as an early birthday present.
4. **SP** "**We** really hope that you enjoy caving," said Kembe's parents as he unwrapped a headlamp.
5. **OP** "It has given **me** a real appreciation for the beauty of the natural world," added Mr. Ly.
6. **PP** Kembe and his dad have traveled to sixteen different states to pursue **their** hobby, but Kembe's mom prefers to stay home.
7. **OP** She has claustrophobia, and tight places make **her** uncomfortable.
8. **SP** **She** has a hard time understanding why Kembe and Mr. Ly love exploring underground.
9. **SP** "**It** is hard to explain," Mr. Ly admits.
10. **PP** "**Our** trips to explore hidden places are just so exciting!" adds Kembe.

13

Page 14

Complete It
Read the passage below. Circle the correct pronoun from each pair in parentheses.

Have (you/we) ever visited Linville Caverns in the mountains of western North Carolina? If you are ever in the area, (its/it) is definitely worth a trip. (Their/Your) guide is likely to tell the group about two teenage boys who explored the caverns on (our/their) own in the early 1900s. The duo was not dressed for the cool 52-degree temperature of the caverns. They eagerly explored the caves with only a lantern to guide (them/him) through the pitch-dark maze. Today, visitors tread on comfortable walkways, and ropes guide them away from the chilly underground stream. This wasn't always the case, though, and the foolish boys were unprepared for the rocky paths.

At one point, the boy holding the lantern dropped and broke (its/it). He and (his/her) partner were left in such darkness that (their/they) could not see their own hands six inches from (their/our) faces! Can (us/you) imagine the panic you'd feel? Luckily, the boys discovered that if they put their hands in the stream, they could detect which way (he/it) flowed. (Them/They) knew that it eventually flowed out of the caverns, so they would need to move in the direction the water was flowing. It took (him/them) two days, but they finally traveled the 800 feet to the cave's entrance. They had hypothermia, and it took them a while to recover, but the boys were lucky to have lived to tell the tale!

Try It
Write several sentences about a place you've explored. Circle each pronoun you use.

Answers will vary.

14

Page 15

Intensive and **reflexive pronouns** are pronouns that end in *-self* or *-selves*. The way the pronoun is used determines whether it is intensive or reflexive.

Intensive pronouns usually appear right after the subject of a sentence. They emphasize the subject.
I *myself* am planning to run the 5K on New Year's Day.
She *herself* is going to repaint the entire interior of the house.
Reflexive pronouns appear elsewhere in the sentence and refer back to the subject.
The rabbit scratched *itself* and then hopped into the garden.
We gave *ourselves* a few extra minutes to get ready before the performance.

Complete It
Complete each sentence below with a reflexive or an intensive pronoun.

1. I **myself** have never visited a library I didn't love.
2. Kaylie gave **herself** a haircut when she was only three, and her mother was not pleased.
3. You and Elijah can make the pizza dough **yourselves** if you have enough time.
4. Jackson read to **himself** all afternoon, and then he took a nap.
5. They **themselves** weren't sure what was going on when the tornado touched down.
6. The team captain **himself or herself** gave a speech after the final game of the season.
7. I asked **myself** over and over again if I had made the right decision.
8. The teacher **himself or herself** bought most of the books on the shelf in the classroom.
9. My father used to tell me that if I wanted to succeed in life, I needed to believe in **myself**.
10. My grandparents **themselves** took care of all the crops and all the animals on the farm.

15

Page 16

Identify It
In each sentence below, the intensive or reflexive pronoun is boldface. Underline the subject the pronoun refers to.

1. The day before the yard sale, <u>Henry</u> **himself** moved fourteen boxes out of the attic.
2. <u>His younger brother and sister</u> helped **themselves** to the things that they felt attached to.
3. There was an old wooden wagon that <u>Mr. Waxhaw</u> **himself** had used when he was first learning how to walk.
4. One box contained quilts that <u>Henry's grandmother</u> had made **herself**.
5. On the day of the sale, it was hot outside, but the <u>attic</u> **itself** was sweltering.
6. <u>June and Xander,</u> Henry's siblings, sprayed **themselves** with a water bottle to keep cool.
7. "Did <u>you</u> **yourself** collect all these cards?" a customer asked Henry, pointing to a collection of baseball cards.
8. "<u>I</u>'m actually not that interested in baseball **myself**," replied Henry. "They were my uncle's cards."
9. At the end of the day, <u>Henry's parents</u> congratulated **themselves** on a clean attic.
10. "<u>We</u> should treat **ourselves** to dinner out with the money we earned!" suggested Mr. Waxhaw.

Try It
Write four sentences using intensive and reflexive pronouns. Circle the intensive pronouns and underline the reflexive pronouns.

1. _____
2. _____
3. _____ Answers will vary.
4. _____

16

Indefinite pronouns are pronouns that do not specifically name the noun that comes before it.

another anybody anyone anything each everybody everyone
everything nobody none no one nothing one somebody someone

I handed my keys to *someone* behind the counter.
Each of my relatives has dark hair.
Everyone leaves through the door on the right.

Most indefinite pronouns are singular, but the following are plural:

both few many others several

Several of the books were donated to the library.
Few visit the zoo on days when it is pouring rain.

Some indefinite pronouns, such as *all, any, more, most,* and *some,* are either singular or plural, depending on their meaning in the sentence.

All is revealed at the end of the book.
All of the children are coming to the party.

Identify It
Underline the indefinite pronoun in each sentence.

1. <u>Everybody</u> loves vacationing at the beach, right?

2. If there is <u>anything</u> troubling you, Shawna, let me know.

3. Keith knocked at the door, but <u>nobody</u> answered.

4. <u>Somebody</u> left a note about finding a lost dog in the park.

5. When Lani got to school, the doors were locked because <u>no one</u> else had arrived yet.

6. The free samples of lotion had already been taken by <u>others</u>, so I went home empty-handed.

7. <u>All</u> of the trees in that lot were chopped down last fall.

8. <u>Both</u> of the kittens pounced at the string.

9. Rex didn't want <u>any</u>, so he politely said, "No, thank you."

10. When the band finally came onstage at midnight, <u>many</u> had already gone home.

17

Complete It
Complete each sentence by circling the correct form of the verb shown in parentheses.

1. When everybody (leave, **leaves**) tonight, please make sure you turn out the lights.

2. All of us (**need**, needs) to be aware of how much energy we use.

3. Nothing (**is**, are) as hard to imagine as a world without oil or coal.

4. However, both (is, **are**) nonrenewable resources.

5. Until somebody (discover, **discovers**) a free, unlimited energy source, we will need to be careful about the energy we use.

6. Everyone (**has**, have) a responsibility to take care of our planet.

7. Today, few (**disagree**, disagrees) with the idea that wind power and solar power are cleaner energy options.

8. Either (create, **creates**) energy with less pollution than coal or oil.

9. Neither (**is**, are) a perfect solution, but each (**is**, are) a better option than using fossil fuels.

Try It
Choose four indefinite pronouns, and write a sentence using each. At the end of each sentence, write **S** if the pronoun is singular and **P** if it is plural.

1. _____

2. _____

3. ___ *Answers will vary.* ___

4. _____

18

A **pronoun shift** happens when a writer changes pronouns in the middle of a sentence or paragraph. This can confuse the reader.

In this example, the writer changes from *they* (third-person plural) to *you* (second-person singular):

Incorrect: When people visit the Statue of Liberty, *they* are often disappointed to learn that *you* are not allowed to walk all the way up to the torch.

Correct: When people visit the Statue of Liberty, *they* are often disappointed to learn that *they* cannot walk all the way up to the torch.

In this example, there is no agreement between *fences* (a plural noun) and *it* (third-person singular pronoun).

Incorrect: The farmer built tall *fences* around his fields because *it* will help keep deer from eating his crops.

Correct: The farmer built tall *fences* around his fields because *they* will help keep deer from eating his crops.

Proof It
Rewrite each sentence to correct the pronoun shift.

1. A professional pianist must practice every day if they want to succeed.
   A professional pianist must practice every day if he or she wants to succeed.

2. A child under the age of 13 needs to be accompanied by their parents.
   A child under the age of 13 needs to be accompanied by his or her parents.

3. Linh and Sammi invited us to go with her to the movies.
   Linh and Sammi invited us to go with them to the movies.

4. Scientists understand that even when an experiment fails, you can still learn something.
   Scientists understand that even when an experiment fails, they can still learn something.

5. A patient surfer will wait for just the right wave before they stand up and ride to shore.
   A patient surfer will wait for just the right wave before he or she stands up and rides to shore.

6. Most students understand that studying hard will help you get good grades.
   Most students understand that studying hard will help them get good grades.

19

Complete It
Circle the pronoun that correctly completes the sentence.

1. The committee met last night, and (**it**, they) decided to approve the new soccer field.

2. When my brother and I got home, (he, **we**) made sandwiches together.

3. Grace and Jacob were nervous because (we, **they**) had never performed in front of a crowd.

4. After the storm, earthworms emerged from the ground, and (it, **they**) began crawling across the sidewalk.

5. If a student must wait for the bus in the dark, be sure to give (**him or her**, them) a flashlight.

6. A new chef faces challenges, but with hard work, (**she**, you) can become successful.

7. The movers struggled to get the piano up the stairs, but at last (we, **they**) got the piano into the music room.

8. After two years, construction for the new garden center was completed last week, and (**it**, they) will finally open on Saturday.

9. The words in the book were printed very small, but I could still read (it, **them**).

10. When people order pizza by phone, (you, **they**) can choose to have the pizza delivered or go pick it up.

11. When singers join this choir, (you, **they**) will often get to perform in different places around the city.

12. Many people go on vacation in August because the weather is nice and (**their**, your) kids don't have to be back in school yet.

Try It
On the lines below, write a short description about a place you would like to visit, including what the experience would be like. Circle each pronoun you use, and proofread your paragraph to be sure there are no pronoun shifts.

_____

___ *Answers will vary.* ___

_____

20

Answer Key

Review: Common and Proper Nouns, Collective and Abstract Nouns, Plurals and Possessives, Appositives

Identify the underlined word using the key in the box. Write your answer on the line following each underlined word.

a. common noun	b. proper noun	c. collective noun	d. abstract noun

1. Desmond's family __a__ moved to Cleveland __b__, Ohio, when Mrs. Otto took a job with NASA __b__.

2. One of Becca's __b__ favorite memories of her childhood __d__ is visiting relatives __a__ in Spain __b__ and befriending a colony __c__ of cats that lived near the wharf __a__ in a seaside town.

3. Chloe opened the Sweet Tooth Bake Shop __b__ last April __b__ because she loves to see the delight __d__ and pleasure __d__ on children's faces when they get to choose a treat.

4. In her carry-on bag __a__, Ms. Tanaka packed a book, a pack __c__ of cards, an overnight kit, one outfit, and an extra pair __c__ of shoes.

In the sentences below, circle singular possessives, underline plurals, and underline plural possessives twice.

1. Mr. (Gillingham's) students are entering their science projects in a citywide science fair.

2. The students' parents will drive them to the auditorium downtown.

3. (Ryan's) project, a 3D model of the sun, took him two weeks to construct.

4. The Wong twins' volcano produces lava and spews tiny rocks.

5. The project we think will win shows how different kinds of stress affect people's bodies.

One sentence above contains an appositive. Write the appositive on the line below.

a 3D model of the sun

21

Review: Personal Pronouns, Intensive and Reflexive Pronouns, Indefinite Pronouns, Pronoun Shifts

Underline the word that best completes each sentence below.

1. Although Jane and Gabriela are best friends, (them, they) do have frequent disagreements.

2. I (myself, yourself) do not enjoy watching scary movies at all.

3. The students who are going to France this summer must work on their French if (you, they) hope to be understood.

4. Morgan and Matt decided that they would throw a surprise birthday party for (them, their) little sister.

5. Mom decided to treat (herself, itself) to a movie and a cup of coffee with (she, her) sister.

6. Uncle Zach and (me, I) are going to stop at the grocery store before (we, they) start dinner.

7. Each of the giraffes cautiously (visit, visits) the watering hole for a drink.

8. When your sisters arrive at the party, tell (them, her) to call me.

9. Micah (itself, himself) will be delivering the gift boxes to all his customers.

10. Both the principal and the vice principal (think, thinks) that students should attend school year-round.

Identify the underlined pronoun in each sentence as a subject pronoun (**SP**), object pronoun (**OP**), or possessive pronoun (**PP**).

1. __PP__ Our puppy is not housetrained quite yet.

2. __SP__ Someone keeps leaving the kitchen light on.

3. __SP__ They will be attending the 9:00 performance.

4. __OP__ Willa wanted them to turn down their music.

5. __PP__ Carter wants to borrow your baseball mitt.

6. __OP__ Josiah dropped something on the bus.

7. __PP__ I hope that you'll be able to come to my graduation.

8. __OP__ My piano teacher asked us to arrive a little early.

22

Action verbs tell the action of the sentence. The action can be physical or mental.

Shawn *jumped* to catch the ball (physical action)
I *hope* your painting wins first place in the art show. (mental action)
Please *sharpen* your pencils before the exam begins. (physical action)
Huang *feels* lousy this morning. (mental action)
Mr. Cooper *framed* the picture using old scraps of wood. (physical action)
Our cat *understands* that whistling means it is time for dinner. (mental action)

Action verbs may also be in past, present, or future tense.

A strong wind *lifted* our kites into the sky. (past)
A strong wind *lifts* our kites into the sky. (present)
A strong wind *will lift* our kites into the sky. (future)

Complete It

Complete each sentence with an action verb. There may be more than one correct answer, but the action verb you choose should make sense in the sentence.

Answers may vary. Possible answers:

1. A campfire __burned__ brightly enough to be seen from several miles away.

2. My mother __said__ we are going to sell a lot of muffins at the bake sale today.

3. Thursday morning, Mrs. Steinfeld __brought__ several bags of clothing to the thrift store.

4. Some old postcards __show__ silly images of people riding giant animals.

5. Karl __sped__ past his opponents.

6. Along the shore, ocean waves __rolled__ over the sand and onto my feet.

7. The trees along the edge of the woods __swayed__.

8. Xavier __wrote__ about the stars and planets.

9. Mongo the Magician __pulled__ a coin from behind his ear.

10. The periodic table __contains__ a lot of information about chemical elements.

11. Uncle Steve __built__ several custom bikes for my cousins and me.

12. I __avoid__ soda because it has too much sugar.

23

Identify It

Read each sentence below. Underline action verbs that describe a physical action. Circle action verbs that describe a mental action.

1. At school yesterday, we discussed the region of Lapland.

2. (think) Lapland is part of Norway, Finland, and Sweden.

3. Long ago, nomads traveled across the region in search of reindeer.

4. Lapps made their clothing from reindeer skins.

5. They preserved reindeer meat by drying or smoking it.

6. Domesticated reindeer pulled sleds and carriages.

7. (remember) my teacher saying Lapps are called the Sami people today.

8. Some Sami people still herd reindeer in the 21st century.

9. Because of reindeers' thick coats, they (prefer) cold temperatures.

10. The subarctic climate of Lapland provides plenty of cold weather for them!

11. The zoo exhibits a small herd of reindeer in a special building.

12. (hope) I get a chance to visit Lapland someday.

Try It

Write one sentence each *Answers may vary. Possible answers:* below.

achieved	change	inspired	will provide	remembered

1. We achieved our goal of winning the State Championship.

2. Sometimes I change my mind about what I want to do after school.

3. The speaker inspired us to become better citizens.

4. The library will provide a free tote bag.

5. She remembered to lock the back door.

24

Spectrum Language Arts
Grade 7

Answer Key

Answer Key

Subject-verb agreement means that the verb must agree in number with the subject of the sentence. If the subject is singular, use a singular verb. If the subject is plural, use a plural verb.

> The <u>pinecone</u> *falls* from the tree.   The <u>pinecones</u> *fall* from the tree.

When a sentence contains a compound subject connected by the word *and*, use a plural verb.

> Desiree **and** Allison *place* all the chairs beside the pool.

When a sentence contains a compound subject connected by the words *or* or *nor*, use a verb that agrees with the subject that is closer to the verb.

> Neither the monkey **nor** her <u>babies</u> *eat* the leaves from that tree.
> Either the girls **or** <u>Samir</u> *sweeps* the kitchen.

If the subject and the verb are separated by a word or words, be sure that the verb still agrees with the subject.

> The <u>camera</u>, as well as the CDs, *is* lost.

Complete It
Complete each sentence below with the correct form of the verb in parentheses.

1. Carlos ___collects___ coins from around the world. (collect)
2. His uncle ___travels___ often for work. (travel)
3. Uncle Pablo and Aunt Maria ___send___ Carlos coins from every place they visit. (send)
4. Carlos's collection ___takes___ up quite a bit of space in his room. (take)
5. Neither his mother nor his brothers ever ___touch___ it. (touch)
6. Carlos ___cleans___ his collection carefully once a week. (clean)
7. The coins ___gleam___ in the sunlight from the window. (gleam)
8. Carlos's brothers ___plan___ to buy Carlos several new coins for his birthday. (plan)
9. They ___find___ a great collector's shop downtown. (find)
10. Their savings ___buy___ three unique coins for Carlos. (buy)

25

Proof It
Read each sentence below. If the subject and verb agree, make a check mark on the line. If they do not agree, use proofreaders' marks to make the necessary corrections.

> ‿ - deletes a word
> ^ - inserts a word

1. _____ Aaron and his friends enjoy~s~ collecting things.
2. _____ Aaron ha~ve~ ^has^ a collection of more than two hundred vintage stamps.
3. _✓_ His uncles, Clark and Will, are also philatelists, or stamp collectors.
4. _____ Neither Aaron nor his uncle~s~ collects contemporary stamps.
5. _✓_ Meghan looks for unusual rocks to add to her collection.
6. _✓_ The rocks can be common or rare, but they must be beautiful.
7. _____ Amina and Jade collect~s~ small glass figures.
8. _____ Amina, and sometimes her mother, ~lies~ ^likes^ to look for the figures at flea markets.
9. _____ Hiromi and his older brother searche~s~ for vinyl records at yard sales.
10. _____ Shelves of records fill~s~ Hiromi's closet.
11. _✓_ Kerry purchases comic books online for her collection.
12. _____ Both Kerry and Owen prefer~s~ buying used comic books.
13. _✓_ Kerry, as well as her older brothers, has been collecting books for more than five years.

Try It
Do you enjoy collecting something? If not, what kind of collections do you think are interesting? Write several sentences about collecting. Make subjects and verbs agree.

> Answers will vary.

26

Transitive verbs are action verbs that are incomplete without a direct object.

> Lydia *picked* <u>some flowers</u>.

Lydia picked is not a complete sentence. The transitive verb *picked* needs a direct object (some flowers) to complete the sentence. Picked what? Some flowers.

> Malik *threw* <u>the ball</u> to his sister.

In this sentence, the transitive verb *threw* needs a direct object (the ball) to complete the sentence. Threw what? The ball.

Intransitive verbs are action verbs that do not have a direct object.

> The girls *ran* across the field.

Identify It
Read each sentence below. Underline transitive verbs once and intransitive verbs twice. For each transitive verb, circle the direct object.

1. The music <u><u>pounded</u></u> loudly in Finnegan's ears.
2. Mrs. Nguyen <u>tasted</u> (the soup) in the large copper pot.
3. Judge Robards <u>sentenced</u> (the criminal) to six years in prison.
4. Cody <u><u>voted</u></u> in the last election for the first time ever.
5. Thea <u>told</u> (a joke) at the beginning of her presentation to the class.
6. Grandpa <u><u>remained</u></u> on the porch late into the evening.
7. Mitzi <u><u>roosted</u></u> all night beside her sisters in the coop.
8. Oliver <u>scribbled</u> (a poem) on the back of his notebook.
9. Dad <u><u>squealed</u></u> to a stop at the red light.
10. The crumbling old letter <u><u>vanished</u></u> into thin air.
11. Dr. Selznick <u>referred</u> (her patient) to a specialist.
12. Have you <u>painted</u> (a portrait) of Madeline yet?

27

Rewrite It
The verb in each sentence below appears in boldface. On the line, write **T** if it is a transitive verb and **I** if it is intransitive. Then, rewrite the sentence using the verb in the opposite way.

> Answers may vary. Possible answers:

> Example: I T ...
> ... ~~she has basketball practice.~~

1. _I_ Joseph **walks** for miles along the beach each evening.
   Joseph walks the dog each morning.
2. _T_ The boys **played** hide-and-seek in the park all afternoon.
   The boys play in the park.
3. _I_ Although she has just started taking lessons, Belle **draws** beautifully.
   Belle draws a horse.
4. _I_ The puppy **drank** thirstily after a long hike in the nature preserve.
   I drank water after jogging around the block.
5. _T_ Zack's temper tantrum **spoiled** the party for his family and friends.
   Leftover meatloaf spoiled before we could eat it.
6. _T_ Mrs. Abdul **washed** the grapes thoroughly in the sink.
   I washed and then went to bed.
7. _T_ Brianna **whispered** a secret in her best friend's ear.
   I whispered to my best friend.
8. _T_ Caleb **studied** after dinner each night before the examination.
   Dr. Wayne studied the report.

Try It
Write ... ... s below.

> Answers may vary. Possible answers:

Trans... ... sail, dig

Intransitive verbs: arrive, laugh
We will sail a ship to Bermuda next year.
The pirates dig sand from the hole.
We arrive at home after six.
Children laugh when they see the clown.

28

Helping verbs help form the main verb in a sentence. Forms of the verbs *be, have,* and *do* are the most common helping verbs.

I **have** started the next book in the series.
Haley **is** playing the lead in the school production of "Annie."

Other helping verbs are *can, could, will, would, may, might, shall, should,* and *must.*

Linking verbs connect a subject to a noun or adjective. They do not express an action. The most common linking verbs are forms of the verb *to be,* such as *is, are, was, were, been,* and *am.*

I *am* happy that you won the spelling bee!
The girls *were* excited about the dance.

Other common linking verbs relate to the five senses (*smell, look, taste, feel, sound*) or a state of being (*appear, seem, become, grow, remain*).

This sushi *tastes* fresh and delicious!
Lauren's eyes *appear* larger behind her glasses.

Identify It
In each sentence below, circle the verb. On the line, write **LV** or **HV** to identify it as a linking verb or helping verb.

1. _LV_ Mary Cassatt (was) a famous Impressionist painter.
2. _LV_ Cassatt's paintings of mothers and children (seem) soft and gentle.
3. _HV_ Cassatt (had) learned a lot about materials and technique from her friend Edgar Degas.
4. _HV_ At the time, few women (could) pursue careers outside the home.
5. _LV_ Cassatt (was) frustrated by the narrow roles of women in society.
6. _HV_ Cassatt's parents (would) argue with their daughter.
7. _HV_ In Paris, Cassatt (could) paint with confidence.
8. _LV_ In Cassatt's paintings, the subjects (appear) very natural and at ease.

29

Complete It
Read the selection below. Underline a linking verb or helping verb to complete the sentences.

People all around the world eat foods that might (seem, remain) bizarre or strange to us. The only way most Americans (could, would) eat a bug is on accident. Insects, however, (is, are) a nutritious source of protein for people in many cultures. Even in America, insects are (becoming, appearing) more popular as a sustainable choice of food. You (should, may) be surprised to learn that the practice of eating insects (have, has) a name—entomophagy. Insects (are, is) plentiful, and many are high in protein as well as vitamins and nutrients like iron, zinc, potassium, and calcium.

The witchetty grub is popular among the aborigines of Australia. When it (has been, have been) cooked, the skin (sounds, tastes) like roast chicken. When the grubs are raw, they (had, have) an almond flavor. If you are interested in trying a buggy snack, you (might, will) consider grasshoppers. Does it (appear, seem) odd to think of eating these long-legged critters? In Mexico, roasted grasshoppers are a crunchy treat. When flavored with garlic, lime, juice, and salt, they (remain, become) tasty and flavorful. Try them, and you (could, should) find that you become a fan of eating bugs. It (appears, sounds) that seeing insects on a menu may (have, be) a common occurrence in the near future.

Try It
What odd, unusual, or interesting foods have you tried? Write a short paragraph about your experience. Underline linking verbs and circle helping verbs in your paragraph.

Answers will vary.

30

Gerunds, participles, and **infinitives** are other kinds of verbs. These verbs take the role of another part of speech in some circumstances.

A **gerund** is when a verb is used as a noun. A verb can take the form of the noun when the ending *–ing* is added.

Skiing is a great way to get outside and enjoy the winter weather.
(The subject *skiing* is a noun in the sentence.)

A **participle** is when a verb is used as an adjective. A verb can take the form of an adjective when the endings *–ing* or *–ed* are added.

The *crumbling* stones showed just how ancient the structure was.
(*crumbling* modifies *stones*)
The *stacked* boxes reached nearly to the ceiling.
(*stacked* modifies *boxes*)

An **infinitive** is when a verb is used as a noun, adjective, or adverb. A verb can take the form of a noun, adjective, or adverb when preceded by the word *to.*

To swim in the ocean is a delightful experience.
(The verb *to swim* acts as the subject, or noun, of the sentence.)
The best way *to travel* is by taking a train.
(The verb *to travel* acts as an adjective modifying *way.*)
I studied all night *to prepare* for the exam.
(The verb *to prepare* acts as an adverb modifying *studied.*)

Complete It
Complete each sentence with a word or phrase from the box. Then, place a **G** for gerund, a **P** for participle, or an **I** for infinitive on the line following the sentence to identify which was used to complete the sentence.

to drink	hanging	to capture
flapping	to lick	planting

1. _To capture_ a photo of a hummingbird can be quite difficult. _I_
2. The _Flapping_ wings of a hummingbird are almost invisible. _P_
3. Hummingbirds like _to drink_ nectar from flowers. _I_
4. Hummingbirds use their long tongues _to lick_ the nectar. _I_
5. _Planting_ the right kinds of flowers will bring hummingbirds to your yard. _G_
6. You can plant the flowers in a _hanging_ basket. _P_

31

Identify It
Read the paragraph below. Underline each gerund once, underline each participle twice, and circle each infinitive.

Each kind of hummingbird has evolved (to survive) in a specific habitat. Chopping down trees or otherwise destroying these habitats is the greatest threat faced by hummingbirds today. Climate change is a problem as well, causing temperatures around the world (to change). The result is altered migratory patterns, and the affected species fly to the wrong places. The birds struggle (to find) food. However, growing the right flowers in your garden will entice the hummingbirds (to visit) your yard and provide them with something to eat. Feeding hummingbirds is a helpful way (to enjoy) nature!

Try It
Make a list of six verbs. Write them on the lines below. Then, change them to gerunds, participles, and infinitives and use them in sentences. Write your new sentences on the lines provided.

Answers will vary.

32

Page 33

A **present tense** verb describes an action that is happening now or happens regularly.
The kittens *play* with a scrap of wrapping paper that fell to the floor.
The DJ *plays* my favorite song at least once a day.

A present tense verb can also express a generalization or fact.
The Bill of Rights *guarantees* each citizen will have certain freedoms.

A **past tense** verb describes an action that happened in the past. For many verbs, the past tense is formed by adding –ed to the base form of the verb.
The maestro *conducted* the orchestra.
The merchants at the market *dismantled* their booths before heading home.

For some verbs, the past tense is a different word.
Emile *taught* his students how to draw using correct perspective. (past tense of *teach*)
Construction *began* last week on the new art center downtown. (past tense of *begin*)

A **future tense** verb describes a future action. The word **will** is used before the verb.
The train *will arrive* in Istanbul tomorrow morning.

Rewrite It
Rewrite each sentence using the indicated tense.

1. Feedback echoed through the auditorium as the crowd cheered.
   Present tense: __Feedback echoes through the auditorium as the crowd cheers.__
2. Encyclopedias line the shelves of Dr. Noguchi's office.
   Future tense: __Encyclopedias will line the shelves of Dr. Noguchi's office.__
3. My scanner malfunctions whenever I try to use the auto setting.
   Past tense: __My scanner malfunctioned whenever I tried to use the auto setting.__
4. Sculpting tools will be offered for half their normal price.
   Past tense: __: Sculpting tools were offered for half their normal price.__
5. A nuthatch pecked holes in the tree trunk and then flew away.
   Present tense: __A nuthatch pecks holes in the tree trunk and then flies away.__
6. The photograph looks fantastic in that new frame!
   Future tense: __The photograph will look fantastic in that new frame!__

33

Page 34

Proof It
Proofread the following paragraph. Use the proofreading marks to correct mistakes with verb tenses and irregular verbs. Insert the correctly spelled words.

⌐ - deletes a word
∧ - inserts a word

Yesterday, our class will visit the planetarium at the science museum downtown. After we took our seats, the museum's manager, Ms. Sanchez, spoke to us for a few minutes about the importance of studying science in school. Next, she introduced us to Dr. Kipper, the director of the planetarium. Then, the lights dimmed, our seats reclined, and the night sky appeared before our eyes. Astronomy is fascinating! We learned that the nearest star to our solar system is Proxima Centauri. It is more than 4 light years away—not exactly "near!" Dr. Kipper next explained that Venus is the easiest planet to see. Then, he told us more about Venus. Earth and its "sister" planet are both about the same size, have about the same amount of gravity, and are made mostly of rock. However, Venus has very little oxygen. On the next clear night, I will try to look for Venus.

Try It
Write about a recent excursion, such as a family outing to the zoo, a class field trip, or even a visit to the library. Be detailed in your description, and include both present and past tense verbs.

__Answers will vary.__

34

Page 35

Progressive verb tenses describe ongoing, or continuing, actions.

A **present progressive** verb describes an action or condition that is ongoing in the present. A present progressive verb is made up of the present tense of the helping verb *be* and the present participle of the main verb.
The elephant *is eating* hay.
My dogs Friar and Tuck *are playing* in the yard.

A **past progressive** verb describes an action or condition that was ongoing at some time in the past. A past progressive verb is made up of the past form of the helping verb *be* and the present participle of the main verb.
Bella *was practicing* ballet last night.
The trees *were swaying* in the breeze.

Identify It
Underline the progressive verbs in each sentence. Then, write **past** or **present** on the line to identify the progressive verb tense.

1. Nadia <u>is writing</u> a report about Cahokia Mounds in Illinois. __present__
2. Trees <u>are growing</u> too close to the overhead power lines. __present__
3. Citizens <u>were willing</u> to rise up and fight their oppressors. __past__
4. The microscope <u>is magnifying</u> a beetle's antenna. __present__
5. Samuel Clemens <u>was writing</u> under the pseudonym Mark Twain. __past__
6. The stars <u>were shining</u> brightly through the spacecraft's window. __past__
7. Crickets <u>are hopping</u> ahead of me as I walk the trail. __present__
8. Benny <u>is sliding</u> down the banister again. __present__
9. Amelia <u>was carefully dusting</u> each little vase before gently placing it back on the shelf. __past__
10. The firecrackers <u>were exploding</u> overhead and startling my baby brother. __past__
11. Hawks <u>are circling</u> above the chicken coop. __present__
12. A taxi <u>is idling</u> at the curb, ready to carry us to the airport. __present__

35

Page 36

Complete It
Use the past progressive forms of the verbs below to complete the paragraph.

practice	kid	approach	act	breath
wear	laugh	block	try	return
chase	kick	wait	have	save
yell	start	entertain	leap	

Brandon and his friends __were practicing__ soccer behind the athletic center, when suddenly a poodle raced across the field. The dog __was wearing__ a pink tutu, and a tall man in red suspenders __was chasing__ it. He __was yelling__, "Foofy! I __was kidding__! Come back!" The boys __were laughing__ hard because the man wore huge clown shoes and a funny wig. As he ran, the big shoes __were kicking__ up mud behind him, and the wig __was starting__ to fall off. All at once, the man stopped. Foofy __was approaching__ the edge of the field where a fence __was blocking__ her way. She stopped too. Everyone __was waiting__ to see what would happen next. The man explained to Brandon, "We __were entertaining__ at a birthday party in the park, but the kids __were acting__ bored. I turned to Foofy and suggested we should have her jump through a ring of fire! I __was trying__ to be funny, but Foofy __was having__ none of it. Next thing I knew, she __was leaping__ off the stage and headed for this field." The man __was breathing__ hard from all the running. The boys were surprised by what happened next. The man pulled a huge steak out of his pocket! In no time, Foofy __was returning__ at full speed to the man's side. "I __was saving__ this for after the show, but it's all yours now, Foofy." Brandon was relieved to see the man and his dog back together.

Try It
Write three verbs on the lines below. Then, use the present progressive form of each verb in a sentence.

1. _____
2. __Answers will vary.__
3. _____

36

Verb tenses tell when in time something happened. The **present perfect** shows that something happened in the past. The action may still be going on. The present perfect is formed with the present tense of the verb have (*have* or *has*) and a past participle.

Mae *has traveled* to Japan four times.

The **past perfect** shows that an action was completed before another action in the past. It is formed with the verb *had* and a past participle.

The lemurs *had climbed* the fence before they scaled the wall.

The **future perfect** shows that an action will be completed before a future time or a future action. It is formed with the words *will have* and a past participle.

By next week, we *will have raised* more money for the school than we did last year.

Identify It
Read each sentence below. The perfect tense verb appears in boldface. On the line, write **PP** if it is in past perfect, **PRP** if it is present perfect, and **FP** if it is in future perfect.

1. PRP Bianca Rodriguez and her family have **attended** the Logan County Fair every year since they moved to Indiana.

2. PP Mrs. Betty Williams **had won** the contest for best pie six years in a row.

3. PRP Bianca **has entered** her blackberry jam in a contest.

4. PP Her sister Rosa **had expected** to win first place for her piglets last year.

5. PP As a judge, Mr. Rodriguez **will have tasted** more than 30 pies this year!

6. PP Once, the Malleys' lambs **had escaped** through a hole in the fence.

7. FP George Hankey **will have operated** the Ferris wheel for nearly two decades.

8. PRP Slim John's Ragtime Band **has played** at the south stage since the fair first began.

9. PRP Alma and Laura, Bianca's cousins, **have tried** every ride at the fair at least once.

10. PP The rain **had poured** down for hours just before the fair started and the sun peeked out.

37

Rewrite It
Read each sentence. On the line, write the **boldface** verb in the past, present, or future perfect tense. The words in parentheses will tell you which tense to use.

1. Jess and McKenna **ask** _have asked_ more than two hundred people to sign their petition. (present perfect)

2. Principal Jackson **lose** _had lost_ his cell phone at the basketball game. (past perfect)

3. If he runs for class president this year, Logan **run** _will have run_ for office three times. (future perfect)

4. Casey **earn** _had earned_ enough money last year to buy the new bike she wanted. (past perfect)

5. Darius **miss** _has missed_ six days of school because he had his tonsils removed. (present perfect)

6. Both Amanda and Eli **want** _had wanted_ to be yearbook editor, so they decided to share the job. (past perfect)

7. The addition to the gym **cost** _will have cost_ the school nearly half a million dollars by the time it is complete. (future perfect)

8. Keiko **play** _had played_ softball for two seasons before she was injured. (past perfect)

9. The kids in the astronomy club **request** _have requested_ permission for a field trip to Lang's Planetarium. (present perfect)

10. Mr. Schneider **hope** _had hoped_ that there would be more volunteers for the science fair on Friday. (past perfect)

Try It
Write three sentences of your own about activities or hobbies you enjoy or would like to try. Write one in the past perfect, one in the present perfect, and one in the future perfect.

Answers will vary.

38

Review: Action Verbs, Subject-Verb Agreement, Transitive and Intransitive Verbs, Helping and Linking Verbs

Read each sentence below. Then, fill in the blank with the type of verb indicated.

1. Carter bounced the ball against the side of the brick building. action verb: _bounced_

2. Jordan was unhappy the whole way home. helping verb: _was_

3. The room suddenly seems smaller to me. linking verb: _seems_

4. LaTanya decided to apply for an internship this summer. action verb: _decided_

5. Lola has asked you at least four times. helping verb: _has_

6. The glass vase shattered against the kitchen floor. action verb: _shattered_

7. That new perfume smells terrible! linking verb: _smells_

8. I have not started either book yet. helping verb: _have_

9. Mr. Ruben considered Brody's request for a new bike. action verb: _considered_

In the sentences below, circle transitive verbs and underline intransitive verbs.

1. Erik (passed) the ball to his brother.

2. Antonio (rode) his bike to the rec center after school.

3. The cat stretched lazily on the bed.

4. The girls (wove) bracelets for their friends.

5. The fire alarm downstairs wailed loudly.

Complete each sentence below with the correct form of the verb in parentheses.

1. Wolves _howl_ as a signal or a warning. (howl)

2. An adult male wolf _leads_ the pack. (lead)

3. Caves, burrows, and hollow logs _make_ perfect dens for wolves. (make)

4. Neither wolves nor other large predators _are_ liked by ranchers and farmers. (to be)

39

Review: Gerunds, Participles, Infinitives, Verb Tenses, Progressive and Perfect Tenses

Identify the underlined word using the key in the box. Write your answer on the line.

a. gerund	b. participle	c. infinitive

1. a Ever since she was a child, <u>swimming</u> has been Alicia's favorite activity.

2. b The <u>wailing</u> child drew the attention of nearly everyone at the grocery store.

3. b The <u>soaring</u> hawk glided along on air currents in the clear blue sky.

4. c If you want <u>to experience</u> a country fully, you must learn the language.

5. a <u>Waiting</u> has never been one of Dana's strengths.

6. c Derrick tried <u>to measure</u> the board as precisely as possible.

Rewrite each sentence below in the tense indicated in parentheses.

1. (present progressive) The boys hike up the side of the mountain.
   The boys are hiking up the side of the mountain.

2. (past progressive) Sharks circle the wounded dolphin.
   Sharks were circling the wounded dolphin.

3. (past progressive) Tomas practices the violin at 7:00 each night.
   Tomas was practicing the violin at 7:00 each night.

4. (present progressive) I print fifty copies of the election poster.
   I am printing fifty copies of the election poster.

Underline the perfect tense verb in each sentence. On the line, write whether the verb is past, present, or future perfect.

1. Dr. Chandra <u>had explained</u> his theory to the class last week. _past_

2. Meghan <u>has eaten</u> escargots, or snails, four times. _present_

3. Eli <u>will have visited</u> each of the fifty states at least once by the year 2018. _future_

4. We <u>had called</u> everyone on the list of names. _past_

5. The Esgrows <u>have visited</u> the Vietnam Veterans' Memorial every summer. _present_

40

Page 41

An **adjective** is a word that describes a noun or pronoun. It offers more information about the word it modifies. Adjectives often come before the noun or pronoun they describe. They answer the question *What kind? How many?* or *Which one?*
The *heavy* rain beat down upon the *drooping* sunflowers.
Sofia's *shiny black* shoes reflected the *bright* lights of the *sparkling* chandelier.

Proper adjectives are capitalized.
Lola ordered *French* fries with her sandwich.
The *Russian* president appeared in several news articles about the event.

A **predicate adjective** follows a linking verb (a form of the verb *to be, smell, look, taste, feel, sound, appear, seem, become, grow,* or *remain*). A predicate adjective modifies the subject of the sentence.
The apples <u>smelled</u> sweet as Ivana dropped them into her basket.

In this example, *sweet* is a predicate adjective, following the linking verb *smelled*. It modifies *apples*, the subject of the sentence.

Identify It
Underline each common or proper adjective you find. Circle the predicate adjectives.

1. Easter eggs usually come in <u>pretty pastel</u> colors.
2. Picture <u>pink, yellow,</u> and <u>purple</u> eggs nestled into baskets filled with <u>sweet</u> treats and <u>faux</u> grass.
3. <u>Ukrainian</u> eggs, however, are (different).
4. <u>Pysanky</u> are (gorgeous) eggs decorated with <u>folk</u> designs.
5. According to tradition, the eggs are dyed with dyes made from <u>colorful</u> flowers, plants, and berries.
6. <u>Heated</u> beeswax is applied to the egg, and then a layer of color is added.
7. In between each layer of color, more <u>beautiful, intricate</u> designs are added.
8. The egg appears (lumpy) with the <u>beeswax</u> markings.
9. Finally, the <u>entire</u> egg is heated so that the <u>warm</u> wax can be removed.
10. A *pysanka* is (special)—a gift that has been created with care and time.

41

Page 42

Complete It
Each sentence below is mi[ssing] ⬚ each blank with an adjective. When you are d[...] [adjecti]ves you used. There is more than one correct ans[...] [each item.]

Answers may vary. Possible answers:

1. The ___beautiful___ sunset over the lake was (spectacular).
2. The ___nauseating___ smell of rotten eggs quickly filled the house.
3. Ian opened the ___heavy___ book, and the smell of ___new___ paper and ink drifted into the room.
4. Tess sat at the ___old wooden___ desk and rested her feet on the ___furry___ back of her ___huge___ dog.
5. Ramona felt (exhausted) as she watched her ___youngest___ son board the ___yellow___ school bus.
6. Anders collapsed onto the ___creaky___ bed, crying ___alligator___ tears into his pillow.
7. The music sounded (refreshing), like opening the window on ___cool___ day.
8. Tanisha chased the ball down the field, brushing her ___long___ hair from her eyes.
9. The baby grew (restless) as the ___dark___ sky filled with ___glittering___ stars.
10. My sister and I carved the ___massive___ pumpkin, adding a ___snarling___ mouth filled with ___sharp___ teeth.

Try It
Describe the most beautiful or unusual place you've ever visited. Use at least eight adjectives in your description.

Answers will vary.

42

Page 43

Comparative adjectives compare two nouns, and **superlative adjectives** compare three or more nouns.
neat, neater, neatest   ugly, uglier, ugliest   wise, wiser, wisest

For adjectives that end in *y*, change *y* to *i* before adding the suffixes *-er* or *-est*.
silly, sillier, silliest   sunny, sunnier, sunniest

Comparing two nouns:
The store on this side of town is *newer* than the store across town.
The pasta salad looks like a *tastier* dish than the potato salad.

Comparing three or more nouns:
The end of school is the *craziest* time of year.
I want to take the *prettiest* way home.

Comparative and superlative adjectives can also be formed by adding the words *more* (comparative) and *most* (superlative) before the adjective. Use *more* and *most* with longer adjectives that have two or more syllables.
That is the *most expensive* pair of sneakers I've ever seen!
Connor becomes *more curious* about that package every day.

Match It
Draw a line to match the sentence blanks in Column A with the adjectives in Column B.

Column A	Column B
1. Of the three assignments, this one is the ____.	busier
2. The weather today is supposed to be ____ than it was yesterday.	stranger
3. I'll take the ____ of the two classes so I'll finish sooner.	earlier
4. Because of the deadlines, I'm ____ this week than next.	easiest
5. Which of the two movies did you think was ____?	gentler
6. I love spicy foods. I want to order the ____ of the two dishes.	spicier
7. Our new dog is much ____ than the wild puppy we used to have.	milder
8. Out of all the bouquets we saw, I think the one with the tulips is the ____.	creamiest
9. Use my recipe, and you will have the ____ guacamole you've ever tasted.	loveliest

43

Page 44

Complete It
Write the correct form of the adjective in parentheses to complete each sentence below.

1. I am ___more comfortable___ these jeans than in any of my other pants. (comparative of *comfortable*)
2. Aunt Wendy became ___lonelier___ after her two cats passed away. (comparative of *lonely*)
3. The weather on Saturday was the ___loveliest___ we've had in weeks. (superlative of *lovely*)
4. Professor Halliday's lecture about black holes was the ___most interesting___ lecture I've heard this year! (superlative of *interesting*)
5. The water in this tide pool is much ___shallower___ than it is where you are standing. (comparative of *shallow*)
6. Cecile's drawing of the human skeletal system is the ___most precise___ I've ever seen. (superlative of *precise*)
7. Bill has got a wonderful secret recipe for the ___crispiest___ fried chicken you've ever had. (superlative of *crispy*)
8. Detective Tang became ___more suspicious___ each time she saw Roland enter the building. (comparative of *suspicious*)
9. Are the gems that Ramon found ___rarer___ than the ones his brother found? (comparative of *rare*)
10. Jess is ___more compassionate___ about animals since she began working at a veterinary practice. (comparative of *compassionate*)

Try It
Write a sentence following the instruction for e[ach.]

Answers may vary. Possible answers:

1. Use the comparative of *frustrating*.
   Missing the bus was more frustrating than forgetting my lunch.
2. Use the superlative of *narrow*.
   The spelunker almost got stuck in the narrowest section of the cave.
3. Use the comparative of *simple*.
   Mr. Laurie's quizzes are always simpler than Mrs. Tompkins's.
4. Use the superlative of *trustworthy*.
   The most trustworthy person I know is my sister, Inez.

44

Page 45

Adverbs modify, or describe, verbs. An adverb tells how, when, or where an action occurs.

　The audience cheered *wildly*. (tells *how* the audience cheered)
　We arrived at the restaurant *late*. (tells *when* we arrived)
　Max tossed the ball *over* the basket. (tells *where* Max tossed the ball)

Adverbs can also modify adjectives or other adverbs.
　The field of snow was *blindingly* white. (*blindingly* modifies the adjective *white*)
　Mr. Langstrom called our house *unusually* early this morning. (*unusually* modifies the adverb *early*)

Many, but not all, adverbs are formed by adding –*ly* to adjectives.

Intensifiers are adverbs that add emphasis or intensity to adjectives or other adverbs. The following are common intensifiers.

| almost | extremely | just | | nearly | practically | quite | rather |
| really | so | | somewhat | such | too | very |

　Kwan is *too* young to join the varsity swim team.
　The seamstress *quite* carelessly tore a hole in the pants.

Identify It
Circle the adverb or intensifier in each sentence. Underline the word that is being modified.

1. The drivers <u>raced</u> (extremely quickly) around the track's curves.
2. The blackberries ripened to a (deep) <u>purple</u> color.
3. Each contestant (excitedly) <u>approached</u> the prize table.
4. The Big Dipper is (really) <u>easy</u> to spot on a clear night.
5. Lance (accidentally) <u>knocked</u> his funny bone against the chair.
6. Dr. Greta <u>aimed</u> the laser (up) toward the moon.
7. Snow <u>fell</u> (soundlessly) from the sky.
8. Plants <u>grow</u> (so slowly) you cannot see them move.

Page 46

Complete It
Fill in each blank with an ~~adverb~~ shown in the box, either to fill in blanks or for ideas. ~~where~~ you place them in the sentences.

Answers may vary. Possible answers:

too	very	practically	politely	helpfully	truly
lately	quite	initially	happily	mostly	freshly
carefully	originally	outside	desperately	quickly	generously
grumpily	only	barely	much	so	
icily	obviously	especially	profusely	such	
helpfully	reluctantly	gently	eagerly	loudly	

　Very early Wednesday morning, Natasha's alarm rang **loudly**. The noise startled her from a **mostly** dreamy sleep. She was **initially** annoyed, but then she **happily** recalled why she had to arise **so** early. Today, Natasha would begin **generously** volunteering at the local food pantry. The pantry **helpfully** provided meals for those in need. The breakfast shift was **especially** important. A child could get a **freshly** made breakfast before heading to school. Natasha **quickly** dressed and rushed **carefully** down the stairs. The sun **barely** peaked above the horizon, so the sky was **mostly** still dark. Natasha had **originally** planned to bike to the pantry, because it was not **too** far from her home. Then, she looked **outside** at the thermometer hanging **helpfully** near the window. The temperature was **icily** cold at just 22°! Natasha **practically** shivered at the thought of riding in **such** freezing weather. Instead, she trudged **reluctantly** back up the stairs and tapped **gently** at her **much** older brother's door. She heard Walt **grumpily** ask, "What?" But when she **politely** explained why she **desperately** needed a ride, he jumped **eagerly** out of bed. He was **truly** impressed with Natasha and **quite** willing to help. It took **only** a few minutes to drive to the pantry. Natasha thanked her brother **profusely** before heading into the building, a huge grin **obviously** adorning her face.

Try It
Write a short descriptive paragraph about traveling through a desert. Include at least four adverbs in your description.

Answers will vary.

Page 47

Like comparative adjectives, **comparative adverbs** compare two actions.
　Our tennis team played *more skillfully* than their team.
　Lana went to bed *later* than Maurice.

Superlative adverbs compare three or more actions.
　The Larkins' home is the *most beautifully* decorated house on the block.
　The Number 12 bus arrived *soonest*.

Short adverbs are formed using –*er* for comparatives and –*est* for superlatives. Long adverbs use the words *more* or *most*, or for negative comparisons, use *less* or *least*.
　The sun rose *earlier* this morning than it did yesterday.
　The sun rises *earliest* on the morning of the summer solstice.
　Sven yelled *more enthusiastically* than his dad did when the Red Sox won.
　Mr. Kline acted *least enthusiastically* about the win.

Some comparative and superlative adverbs do not follow these patterns. The following are examples of irregular comparative and superlative adverbs.
　well, better, best　　　badly, worse, worst

Rewrite It
Rewrite each sentence below using a comparative or superlative adverb.

1. Claude stared seriously at the unfinished painting.
　comparative: Claude stared more seriously at the unfinished painting.
2. The cardinal flew quietly out of its nest.
　superlative: The cardinal flew most quietly out of its nest.
3. The team of scientists arrives soon.
　comparative: The team of scientists arrives sooner.
4. Frank's Fish was reviewed favorably in our local paper.
　comparative: Frank's Fish was reviewed more favorably in our local paper.
5. I am eagerly awaiting the visit with my Uncle Lenny.
　superlative: I am most eagerly awaiting the visit with my Uncle Lenny.
6. Hanna looked obviously annoyed about the e-mail.
　comparative: Hanna looked more obviously annoyed about the e-mail.
7. Ms. Rain smiled happily when the phone rang.
　superlative: Ms. Rain smiled most happily when the phone rang.

Page 48

Proof It
Proofread the following sentences. Use the proofreading marks to correct mistakes with comparative and superlative adverbs.

1. The monkeys reacted ~~curiousest~~ **most curiously** to the bananas presented on trays.
2. I felt ~~more bad~~ **worse** about missing my brother's swim meet.

| ~~e~~ | – deletes a word |
| ^ | – inserts a word |

3. Mae arranged her clothes ~~less~~ sloppily than Rachel did.
4. Those sheep seem to eat ~~greedier~~ **more greedily** than the pigs.
5. The moon's gravity pulls less ~~stronger~~ **strongly** than Earth's gravity does.
6. Lucy finished her lunch ~~earliest~~ **earlier** than the other students.
7. The builders worked ~~feverisher~~ **more feverishly** when they learned they could earn a bonus.
8. I study ~~most~~ **best** well when I have some quiet music playing.
9. The van was parked ~~more~~ **closer** close to the curb.
10. The hands of the clock move more ~~slowest~~ **slowly** if you feel bored.
11. Mr. Hanson awarded the students who behaved ~~properliest~~ **most properly** during the performance.
12. Darnell's trip to the dentist went ~~smootherer~~ **more smoothly** than he had expected.
13. Oscar traveled most ~~comfortabler~~ **comfortably** when sitting in an aisle seat.
14. At business school, Beth spoke more ~~professionaler~~ **professionally** than she did at home.
15. Of all Stella's animals, the dogs wait ~~leastest~~ **least** patiently.

Try It
Choose six adverbs from the ~~box and write three~~ sentences using the comparative form. For the ~~other three, write~~ sentences using the superlative form.

Answers may vary. Possible answers:

~~quietly~~	~~often~~	~~delicately~~	~~graciously~~	~~sleepily~~
happily	affectionately	eagerly	critically	carelessly
sluggishly			closely	lovingly

1. Mr. Ware looks more critically at the work of older students.
2. We visit the beach more often than the mountains.
3. My dog acts more affectionately toward my brother than me.
4. The downtown library is farthest from my home.
5. Of all the students, William waited most eagerly for the field trip.
6. I handled my egg most carelessly, so my egg was the only one that broke.

Page 49

Some adjectives and adverbs are easy to confuse with one another. Use a predicate adjective after a linking verb (forms of the verb *to be* and verbs like *seem, taste, grow,* and *become*). Use an adverb to describe an action verb.

The music <u>sounded</u> *joyful* as it streamed through the open windows.
Zora <u>played</u> *joyfully,* as though a large audience was listening.

In first example, the adjective *joyful* follows the linking verb *sounded* and modifies the subject *music.* In the second example, the adverb *joyfully* modifies the action verb *played.*

The words *good, well, bad,* and *badly* are often used incorrectly. *Good* and *bad* are adjectives, and *well* and *badly* are adverbs.

Your homemade yogurt <u>tastes</u> *good.*
The milk you bought last week <u>is</u> *bad.*
Daisy <u>behaved</u> *badly* at the groomer's on Friday.
Bubbles and Ringo <u>ate</u> *well* today, even though they were sick last night.

Match It
Match each sentence to the adjective or adverb that completes it. On the line, write the letter of your choice.

1. __a__ The noise was _____ and startled the grackles in the oak tree.
  a. sudden
  b. suddenly

2. __b__ The chipmunk darted _____ across the yard.

3. __b__ Toshi felt _____ as he waited in line at the post office.
  a. impatiently
  b. impatient

4. __a__ Samuel waited _____ while his sister put on her shoes.

5. __a__ Felix watched _____ as his team scored another goal.
  a. eagerly
  b. eager

6. __b__ The children grew _____ as the first snowflake started to fall.

7. __b__ Kara performed _____ after a long, sleepless night.
  a. bad
  b. badly

8. __a__ Joshua felt _____ that he had missed Kara's performance.

9. __a__ Ms. Hennessy appeared _____, but I knew she was nervous.
  a. calm
  b. calmly

10. __b__ Although the weather was rough, the pilot flew _____.

Page 50

Identify It
Read each item below. On the line, write **Adj.** or **Adv.** to identify each boldface word as an adjective or adverb. If the word is an adjective, underline the linking verb it follows. If the word is an adverb, circle the action verb it follows.

1. __Adj__ The pink peony that Elena chose <u>smelled</u> **fragrant**.
2. __Adv__ Mittens (meowed) **cheerfully** at Mia's door at six o'clock in the morning.
3. __Adv__ It rained all night, but the next morning, the sun (shone) **brightly**.
4. __Adj__ The rickety wooden bridge <u>appeared</u> **unsafe**, but Justin decided to take his chances.
5. __Adj__ Although we were in a rural area, our cell phone reception <u>was</u> **good**.
6. __Adj__ Quinn was no expert, but the cheese <u>tasted</u> **rancid**.
7. __Adj__ Aunt Ella <u>looked</u> **elegant** in the cherry red ball gown.
8. __Adv__ Grandma Sheryl claims that she never (sleeps) **well** in a hotel room.
9. __Adv__ The door (closed) **completely**, even before Mickey had finished speaking.
10. __Adv__ O'Connor made the basket, and the crowd (cheered) **wildly**.
11. __Adj__ The auditorium <u>grew</u> **quiet** as Mr. Hague took the stage.
12. __Adv__ After spending most of the day in the car, the boys (acted) **badly** at dinner.

Try It
Write two sentences containing adverbs and two containing adjectives.

1. _____
2. _____
   Answers will vary.
3. _____
4. _____

Page 51

Prepositions are words that show the relationship between a noun or pronoun and another word in the sentence.

The truck ran *off* the road.   The garbage can is *beside* the fence.

Some common prepositions are *above, across, after, along, around, at, away, because, before, behind, below, beneath, beside, between, by, down, during, except, for, from, in, into, near, off, on, outside, over, to, toward, under, until, up, with, within,* and *without.*

Prepositional phrases include the prepositions and the objects (nouns or pronouns) that follow the prepositions. A prepositional phrase includes the preposition, the object of the preposition, and the modifiers of the object. Prepositional phrases tell *when* or *where* something is happening.

The calico cat hid *under the white bookshelf.* (Where? Under the white bookshelf)
Anson woke up *before his brother.* (When? Before his brother)

Complete It
Each sentence below is missing a preposition. Complete the sentences with prepositions from the box. There may be than one correct answer for each item.

for	from	to	with	during
by	around	off	beneath	in

1. An iceberg is a large piece of ice that floats __in__ open water.
2. The word *iceberg* comes __from__ a Dutch word that means "ice mountain."
3. Most of an iceberg lies __beneath__ the water; only about one-tenth is above the water.
4. A dome iceberg is an iceberg __with__ a rounded top.
5. Today, icebergs are monitored __by__ the U.S. National Ice Center.
6. Most icebergs are formed __during__ the spring and summer.
7. An iceberg was responsible __for__ the sinking of the *Titanic.*
8. Even today, icebergs can cause great damage __to__ a ship.
9. Most of the world's icebergs are found __around__ Antarctica and Greenland.
10. When a chunk of ice calves, it breaks __off__ a glacier and an iceberg is formed.

Page 52

Identify It
Underline each prepositional phrase in the sentences below. Circle each preposition. The number in parentheses will tell you how many prepositions each sentence contains.

1. The *Titanic* was a luxury passenger ship that sailed (from) Southampton, England. (1)
2. The awesome ship collided (with) an iceberg. (1)
3. The iceberg came (from) a glacier (in) Greenland. (2)
4. The *Titanic* sank (on) its maiden voyage. (1)
5. The remains (of) the great boat lie more than 12,000 feet (beneath) the ocean's surface. (2)
6. The *Titanic* used 825 tons (of) coal every day. (1)
7. It took 74 years to locate the wreck (of) the *Titanic.* (1)
8. When the *Titanic* set sail, she was the largest human-made moving object (on) Earth. (1)
9. (During) its voyage, the *Titanic* did not hold any lifeboat drills (for) the passengers. (2)
10. (After) the wreck, hundreds (of) stories were written (about) the ill-fated voyage. (3)

Try It
Write a short paragraph about a momentous news event that has occurred during your lifetime. Underline each preposition you use.

_____
_____
Answers will vary.
_____
_____

Conjunctions connect individual words or groups of words in sentences.

Coordinate conjunctions connect words, phrases, or independent clauses that are equal or of the same type. Coordinate conjunctions are *and, but, or, nor, for,* and *yet*.
The satin dress felt smooth *and* silky beneath Anna's fingers.

Correlative conjunctions come in pairs and are used together. *Both/and, either/or,* and *neither/nor* are examples of correlative conjunctions.
Neither Michael *nor* Aiden can join us tonight.

Subordinate conjunctions connect dependent clauses to independent clauses in order to complete the meaning. *After, although, as long as, since, unless, whether,* and *while* are examples of subordinate conjunctions.
Whether it snows or not, we will go to the play tomorrow.

An **interjection** is a word or phrase used to express surprise or strong emotion. Common interjections include:

| ah | alas | aw | awesome | eeek | hey | hi |
| hurray | oh | oh, no | oops | ouch | phew | wow |

An exclamation mark [...] jection to separate it from the rest of the sentence.
Oops! I dropped [...] to hear that!

Answers may vary. Possible answers :

Complete It
Complete each of the following sentences with an interjection of your choosing.

1. __Ow__ ! I burned my hand on the stove!
2. __Darn__ , that is probably the last chance we'll have to talk with Professor Snoddkins.
3. __Wow__ ! That was a close call!
4. __Oh__ , what a beautiful bouquet of tulips!
5. __Yay__ ! I'm so happy all your hard work paid off!
6. __Shoot__ , that's exactly what I thought would happen!

53

Identify It
Read the phrases in the box. Write them beside the appropriate headings.

the ladybugs or the aphids	unless you can find the book
the green and yellow shirts	both the wrench and the hammer
since Pablo left for school after the storm	likes shrimp but hates fish
neither the mangoes nor the kiwis	either on Monday or on Wednesday

Coordinate Conj. _____

Correlative Conj. _____

Answers may vary. Possible answers :

Subordinate Conj. _____

Try It
For each number below, write a sentence that includes the items in parentheses.

1. (a correlative conjunction) _____
Whew! Neither the bee nor the wasp stung me!
2. (a subordinate conjunction) _____
As long as you are in the kitchen, could you please bring me a glass of water?
3. (an interjection) _____
Super!
4. (a subordinate conjunction and a coordinate conjunction) _____
Unless you are too busy, pick up your room and fold the laundry.
5. (an interjection and a correlative conjunction) _____
Hey! Stop at both the library and the grocery store on your way home!
6. (two coordinate conjunctions) _____
Dad's beard and mustache need a trim, but his beard trimmer is broken.
7. (a correlative conjunction) _____
I can get you in to see the doctor at either 11:30 or 12:30.

54

Review: Adjectives and Predicate Adjectives, Comparative and Superlative Adjectives, Adverbs and Intensifiers, Comparative and Superlative Adverbs

Identify the adjective in each sentence. If it is a predicate adjective, underline it. Circle the other adjectives. On the line, write **C** if the adjective is comparative, write **S** if the adjective is superlative, and leave the line blank if the adjective is neither comparative nor superlative.

1. __S__ The (tallest) mountain in the world, measured from its base, is Mauna Koa.
2. _____ You may not recognize the name, but Mauna Koa is _famous_.
3. _____ This mountain is the (beautiful) island of Hawaii.
4. __C__ Mt. Everest, however, is _higher_ above Earth's surface.
5. _____ Mt. Everest towers over the (forbidding) landscape of Tibet.
6. _____ Tenzing Norgay and Edmund Hillary completed the (first) ascent in 1953.
7. _____ The ascent may be _treacherous_, but thousands have climbed to Everest's peak since then.
8. __C__ Considering the mountain's remoteness, the area is _messier_ than you might imagine.
9. _____ (Abandoned) gear lies scattered along the trail to the top.
10. _____ Artists from Nepal came up with a (creative) idea.
11. _____ They turned the (worthless) junk into art!
12. _____ Art galleries were _enthusiastic_ about the idea.

As indicated, rewrite each sentence to change the adverb to a comparative or superlative adverb. If the sentence contains an intensifier, circle the intensifier.

1. [...] he way (almost) out of time.
Comparative: Raj typed more quickly because he was (almost) out of time.
2. Mr. Lincoln was extremely tired this evening, so he trudged sleepily up the stairs.
Comparative: Mr. Lincoln was (extremely) tired this evening, so he trudged more sleepily up the stairs.
3. The kayak raced speedily through the rapids.
Superlative: The kayak raced most speedily through the rapids.
4. My friend plays soccer well when he has had a big breakfast.
Superlative: My friend plays soccer best when he has had a big breakfast.

55

Review: Adjectives and Adverbs, Prepositions and Prepositional Phrases, Conjunctions and Interjections

Circle the correct adjective or adverb to complete each sentence.

1. Mr. Louis feels (bad) badly about missing the performance.
2. The entire class felt (cheerfully, (cheerful)) after a visit from Officer Bunkley.
3. I did (good, (well)) on my algebra test.
4. Nan waited (impatiently) impatient) for the receptionist to call her name.
5. Lying in bed, Brie could hear ((quiet) quietly) raindrops tapping the window.

Identify the boldface word in each sentence. On the line, write **P** if it is a preposition, **C** if it is a conjunction, or **I** if it is an interjection. For sentences that contain a preposition, also underline the prepositional phrase.

1. __I__ **Wow**, you really know how to juggle, don't you?
2. __P__ The robin landed **on** the birdfeeder.
3. __C__ **Whenever** Trent mows the lawn, he also uses the weed whacker.
4. __P__ We will be studying the Civil War **until** the semester ends.
5. __C__ The dog barks all night, **yet** he never sleeps during the day.
6. __I__ **Oops**, I didn't mean to close that window yet.
7. __C__ Rudy **and** his sister will be visiting Atlanta next week.
8. __P__ The Ingalls bought their horses **from** a breeder in Kentucky.
9. __P__ Wind this string **around** the stake at the end of the yard.
10. __C__ Please give this note to Mr. Rickert **while** you are at his office.

Write a sentence that contains two prepositional phrases: _____

Write a sentence that contains a [...]: _____

Answers will vary.

Write a sentence that contains a correlative conjunction: _____

Write a sentence that contains a subordinate conjunction: _____

56

Page 57

A **declarative sentence** makes a statement about a place, person, thing, or idea, and it ends with a period.

    Cirrus clouds look like wispy smears of white in the blue sky.

An **interrogative sentence** asks a question and ends with a question mark.

    Why do airplanes sometimes leave long, white trails through the sky?

An **exclamatory sentence** shows urgency, strong surprise, or emotion, and ends with an exclamation mark.

    That sunset is so beautiful!

An **imperative sentence** demands that an action be performed. The subject of an imperative sentence is usually not expressed, but the subject is normally understood as *you*. Imperative sentences can be punctuated with a period or an exclamation mark.

    Hand me the binoculars, please.
    Look at that funnel cloud!

Answers may vary. Possible answers:

Rewrite It
Rewrite each sentence so it provides an example of the indicated sentence type.

1. Fog is a stratus cloud that has formed at ground level.
    Interrogative: **Is fog a stratus cloud that formed at ground level?**

2. Cumulonimbus clouds can reach heights of 60,000 feet.
    Exclamatory: **Cumulonimbus clouds can reach heights of 60,000 feet!**

3. Can you please grab my book about clouds?
    Imperative: **Please grab my book about clouds.**

4. What does *nimbus* mean when it appears at the end of a cloud name?
    Imperative: **Tell me what *nimbus* means when it appears at the end of a cloud name.**

5. Is *nimbus* the Latin word for "shower"?
    Declarative: ***Nimbus* is the Latin word for "shower."**

6. A "mackerel sky" is known scientifically as cirrocumulus clouds.
    Interrogative: **What is the scientific name for a "mackerel sky"?**

57

Page 58

Identify It
Read the passage below. Use the line following each sentence to identify the sentence type. Write **D** for declarative, **IN** for interrogative, **E** for exclamatory, and **IM** for imperative.

    Turn your eyes to the sky and describe what's there. __IM__ Is it all blue? __IN__ Then, your job will be fairly easy. __D__ How do you describe the different kinds of clouds, though? __IN__ If you're a poet, you're free to use metaphors and other figurative language. __D__ If you're a scientist, you need to be more precise. __D__ In the early 1800s, Englishman Luke Howard devised a system for describing clouds based on their appearances. __D__ He classified clouds into three categories: cirrus, stratus, and cumulus. __D__ Have you ever seen delicate, wispy clouds that look like they were painted onto the sky by a brush? __IN__ Those are cirrus clouds, and they form more than 20,000 feet above the ground. __IN__ That's way up there! __E__

    Stratus clouds are found lower, at an altitude of between 6,000 and 20,000 feet. __D__ Try to guess how stratus clouds look. __IM__ If I gave you a hint, would it help? __IN__ Drizzle or light snow often falls from stratus clouds. __D__ Did you guess that stratus clouds appear as an overcast sky? __IN__ Then, you're right! __E__ When stratus clouds are overhead, it looks like a smooth ceiling of white or gray has moved across the sky. __D__

    So what about big, puffy white clouds drifting through the sky on a summer day? __IN__ Those are cumulus clouds. __D__ They don't usually bring rain, but on a steamy day a cumulus cloud can grow bigger and bigger until it's a cumulonimbus cloud. __D__ Take cover! __E__ A cumulonimbus cloud is also known as a thunderhead, most likely bringing thunder, lightning, and heavy rain as it rolls over the land. __D__

Try It
On the lines below, write one example each of the four sentence types.

Declarative: _____

Interrogative: _____

Exclamatory: _____ *Answers will vary.*

Imperative: _____

58

Page 59

An **independent clause** presents a complete thought and can stand alone as a sentence.

Simple sentences are sentences with one independent clause. Simple sentences can have one or more subjects and one or more predicates.

    The players huddled in the middle of the field. (one subject, one predicate)
    The players and *the coaches* huddled in the middle of the field. (two subjects, one predicate)
    The players and the coaches *huddled in the middle* of the field and *discussed the next play*. (two subjects, two predicates)

Compound sentences are sentences with two or more simple sentences, or independent clauses. A compound sentence can be two sentences joined with a comma and a coordinate conjunction. The most common coordinating conjunctions are *and, but, or, yet,* and *so. For* and *nor* can also act as coordinating conjunctions.

    Eli handed the ball to Terrell, but Terrell fumbled it.

A compound sentence can also be two simple sentences joined by a semicolon.

    Eli handed the ball to Terrell; Terrell fumbled it.

Match It
Match a simple sentence from Column A with a simple sentence from Column B to create a compound sentence. Write each compound sentence on the lines below, and remember to add either a coordinate conjunction or punctuation.

Column A	Column B
1. The first Super Bowl was played in January 1967.	1. The Green Bay Packers were the NFL champions.
2. It featured the best team of the AFL against the best team of the NFL.	2. Bart Starr was named Most Valuable Player.
3. The Kansas City Chiefs were the AFL champions.	3. Some people called it the Supergame.
4. The first half of the game was competitive.	4. The second half would determine the best football team in America.
5. Packers' Quarterback Bart Starr scored two touchdowns and threw for 250 yards.	5. The second half of the game was determined by the Packers.

Answers may vary. Possible answers:

1. The first Super Bowl was played in January 1967; some people called it the Supergame.
2. It featured the best team of the AFL against the best team of the NFL, and the game would determine the best football team in America.
3. The Kansas City Chiefs were the AFL champions, and the Green Bay Packers were the NFL champions.
4. The first half of the game was competitive, but the second half of the game was dominated by the Packers.
5. Packers' Quarterback Bart Starr scored two touchdowns and threw for 250 yards; he was named Most Valuable Player.

59

Page 60

Identify It
Read each sentence and determine whether it is a simple or compound sentence. On the line at the beginning of the sentence, write **S** for simple or **C** for compound. On the two lines following the sentence, identify the total number of subjects and predicates in each sentence.

1. __C__ The referee blew her whistle, and both teams rushed onto the field.
    S: _2_ **P:** _2_

2. __C__ The Western Wildcats and the Northside Knights had played each other earlier in the season, but tonight's game was the regional championship.
    S: _3_ **P:** _2_

3. __S__ Eli took the snap and hurled the ball downfield. **S:** _1_ **P:** _2_

4. __C__ Brandon leaped for the ball, but Jamal was there first. **S:** _2_ **P:** _2_

5. __C__ The crowd roared, jumped to its feet, and then groaned; Jamal could not hold on to the ball, and he dropped it. **S:** _2_ **P:** _5_

6. __C__ The next play was less exciting, for Eli handed off the ball for no gain.
    S: _2_ **P:** _2_

7. __C__ Eli's father yelled and caught the attention of a vendor; she sold him three hot dogs. **S:** _2_ **P:** _3_

8. __C__ Eli had run straight up the middle and scored a touchdown, but his father was buying hot dogs and missed it. **S:** _2_ **P:** _4_

9. __S__ The team grabbed Eli and hoisted him onto their shoulders.
    S: _1_ **P:** _2_

10. __S__ They carried him back to the sidelines and set him down by the coach.
    S: _1_ **P:** _2_

11. __S__ The coach and several other players gave Eli high-fives. **S:** _2_ **P:** _1_

12. __C__ Eli's father ate the hot dogs, but he didn't buy anything else for the rest of the game. **S:** _2_ **P:** _2_

Try It
Write a paragraph about a sporting event you attended or took part in. Include a variety of simple and compound sentences in your description.

Answers will vary.

60

Page 61

A **dependent clause** does not present a complete thought and cannot stand alone as sentence.

Complex sentences have one independent clause and one or more dependent clauses. The independent and dependent clauses are connected with a subordinate conjunction or a relative pronoun. The dependent clause can be anywhere in the sentence.
Complex sentence (connected with subordinate conjunction):
    The metric system is easy to use *because* the units are based on multiples of 10.
Complex sentence (connected with a relative pronoun):
    I just finished a biography of Muhammad Ali, *who* everybody knows is the greatest boxer of all time.

The dependent clause can either be the first or second part of the sentence.
    Before you can water the garden, you need to turn on the spigot at the house.
    You need to turn on the spigot at the house *before* you can water the garden.

Complete It
For each unfinished complex sentence, choose a subordinate conjunction from the list and use it to write the missing part. Use a different word from the list for each sentence.

after	if	unless	where
although	once	until	wherever
because	since	when	whether
before	though	whenever	while

1. <u>After he gets back from work</u>, Jack will join us for the celebration.
2. The snow fell continuously for nearly three hours <u>while we sat inside by the fire.</u>
3. Dr. Murray emptied the cupboards above the sink <u>because she was moving to a new office.</u>
4. <u>Although the company wanted them</u>, the lumberjacks spent the weekend in town.
5. Most of William's friends ride home on Bus #19 <u>whenever they have the chance</u>.
6. <u>Once it is filled</u>, the garbage truck hauls its load to the dump.
7. <u>When you present them at the party</u>, cupcakes decorated as ladybugs will be a hit!
8. You can't join the Rocky Ridge Nature Club <u>until you are fourteen</u>.
9. Hazel's favorite rollercoaster zips downhill at more than 100 m.p.h. <u>before making a sharp turn</u>
10. <u>While we were at the beach</u>, storm clouds moved quickly across the horizon and blocked the setting sun.

61

Page 62

For each sentence, circle the subordinate conjunction and underline the dependent clause.
1. (Although) its official name is *Cloud Gate*, most Chicagoans refer to Anish Kapoor's famous sculpture as "The Bean."
2. The beautiful mirrored surface is hard to describe (unless) you've seen it in person.
3. Kapoor was born in India in 1954 and lived (until) he moved to Britain in the early 1970s.
4. He was awarded the Turner Prize in 2002, (which) is a very prestigious honor given annually to the best British artist under 50 years old.
5. (Whenever) most people visit Chicago, a trip to see "The Bean" is on their list of things to do.
6. Visitors can walk right under the sculpture (because) the arched shape underneath it is 12 feet high.
7. Be sure to bring a camera (when) you visit.
8. The curved surfaces create distorted reflections (that) make great photographs.
9. (After) you visit "The Bean," you can find other interesting activities nearby.
10. (Since) the sculpture is located in Millennium Park, you'll have just a short walk to ice-skating, gardens, and another fun public artwork, *Crown Fountain*.
11. (Although) *Crown Fountain* is a piece of art, it's also a place to play.
12. Water cascades down the 50-foot tall glass walls of the fountain (while) LED lights behind the glass project videos.
13. (Unless) it's a really cold day, visitors play in the water falling down the wall and collecting in a pool at the base.
14. I recommend a visit to Chicago's Millennium Park (if) you get the chance.
15. (Whether) you like dancing in fountains, ice-skating, or seeing great public art, you're sure to enjoy it.

Try It
Write five complex sentences on the lines below. Use subordinate conjunctions in four of the sentences and a relative pronoun in the fifth sentence.
1. _____
2. _____
3. _____ Answers will vary.
4. _____
5. _____

62

Page 63

An **adjective clause** is a dependent clause that modifies a noun or pronoun. An adjective clause usually follows the word it modifies. The clause begins with a relative pronoun, such as *that, which, who, whom,* or *whoever*.
    Mira's sister, *who you saw at a dance recital*, sprained her ankle.
    Cockroaches carry bacteria *that may cause food poisoning*.

An **adverb clause** is a dependent clause that modifies a verb, an adjective, or an adverb. An adverb clause answers the question *How? When? Where? Why?* or *Under what condition?* The first word of an adverb clause is a subordinate conjunction, such as *although, until, once, however, unless, if,* or *while*.
    Until Grandpa retires, he will continue to get up at 5:30 A.M.
    I'll walk to school tomorrow *if it isn't raining.*

Complete It
Each boldface adjective clause below is missing a relative pronoun. Each boldface adverb clause is missing a subordinate conjunction. Choose a relative pronoun or subordinate conjunction from the box and write it on the line to complete the sentence.

Relative Pronouns

whom	which	that	whoever	who

Subordinate Conjunctions

when	unless	if	whenever	while

1. The moonflower, **which is a member of the morning glory family**, blooms in the evening.
2. You will miss Justin's speech **if you don't hurry**.
3. The girl **when won the spelling bee is in her class.**
4. Emil volunteers at the food bank **when he has the time**.
5. It is unusual for rain to fall **while the sun is out**.
6. Sadie is a friend **whom you've met** several times.
7. Roasted chickpeas are a crunchy treat **that you would like**.
8. **Unless you are an expert in edible plants**, it is best not to eat things that grow in the wild.
9. **Whenever we go to the market**, Mom buys fresh goat cheese.
10. The person with muddy feet, **whoever that may be**, needs to clean the floors.

63

Page 64

Identify It
Read the sentences below. Circle the adjective clauses, and underline the adverb clauses.
1. African wild dogs, (which live south of Africa's Sahara Desert), are similar to wolves.
2. <u>Although they are called "dogs,"</u> these animals are definitely wild, not domesticated.
3. <u>Since African wild dogs have unique patterns,</u> it is easy to distinguish them from one another.
4. Dr. McNutt, (who studies African wild dogs), hopes to educate people about these rare and unusual animals.
5. <u>Whereas there are millions of domestic dogs,</u> only about 6,000 wild African dogs remain.
6. Something must be done <u>before the numbers of wild dogs sinks even lower.</u>
7. <u>Because they are fast runners,</u> wild dogs can hunt animals like gazelles, antelope, and birds.
8. Wild dogs (that attack cows and sheep on ranches) may be shot.
9. Ranch owners, (whose livelihood depends on their livestock), have little patience for wild dogs.
10. The sounds wild dogs make are meaningless <u>unless you know what to listen for.</u>

Try It
Why are wild animals worth saving? Write several sentences about your views. Circle the adjective clauses and underline the adverb clauses in your answer.

_____
_____
Answers will vary.
_____
_____

64

Page 65

Review: Sentence Types, Simple and Compound Sentences

Read the sentences below. Use the line following each sentence to identify the sentence type. Write **D** for declarative, **IN** for interrogative, **E** for exclamatory, and **IM** for imperative.

1. Are you familiar with the artwork of pop artist Andy Warhol? __IN__
2. If you haven't seen it before, you might be surprised! __E__
3. Andy's mother taught him to draw when he was eight years old and was ill with a liver disease. __D__
4. In 1961, Andy had a unique idea about using mass-produced commercial products in his art. __D__
5. Would you consider an image of a soup can, repeated over and over in different colors, to be art? __IN__
6. Andy also used images of celebrities, such as Marilyn Monroe and Che Guevara, in his artwork. __D__
7. Today, some of Andy Warhol's pieces are worth more than $100 million! __E__
8. Go see Andy's artwork in person if you ever have the opportunity. __IM__

Identify each sentence below as simple (**S**) or compound (**C**).

1. __S__ Andy sometimes told the press fictional stories about his youth.
2. __C__ Andy's last name was originally Warhola, but he later changed it to Warhol.
3. __S__ Andy Warhol aspired to wealth and fame.
4. __C__ Andy wanted his artwork to be available to everyone, so he mass produced it.
5. __S__ Did you know that Andy Warhol also produced films?
6. __C__ The Factory was Andy's studio, but he also held large parties there.
7. __S__ Silk screening and painting were two types of artwork Andy produced.
8. __S__ Andy Warhol loved cats and created many images of them.

65

Page 66

Review: Complex Sentences, Adjective and Adverb Clauses

Underline the dependent clause in each complex sentence below.

1. <u>Although Tanesha lives in California,</u> we often text each other.
2. <u>Whenever we go to a baseball game,</u> my dad buys us popcorn and lemonade.
3. We can visit the Empire State Building <u>before we get together with Grandpa.</u>
4. <u>Unless you brought rain boots with you,</u> we probably shouldn't go for a walk.
5. Rosie gets nervous <u>when she has to speak in front of large groups.</u>
6. <u>Whether or not you've done your homework,</u> there will be a quiz on Thursday.
7. Logan rubbed Crosby's back <u>while the vet gave the dog a shot.</u>
8. <u>After Dr. Hafiz reviewed the test results,</u> she called with the news.

Read the sentences below. Circle the adjective clauses, and underline the adverb clauses.

1. Kiwis, (which are flightless birds) live in New Zealand.
2. <u>Although he loved the Mississippi River,</u> Mark Twain almost drowned in it as a boy.
3. <u>Until Hurricane Katrina made landfall,</u> no one knew what devastation the broken levees would cause.
4. <u>For more than 2,000 years,</u> reindeer have been domesticated.
5. The Statue of Liberty is covered in a layer of copper (that is very thin)
6. Babe Ruth kept an icy cold cabbage leaf under his baseball hat <u>during hot weather.</u>
7. The Kingda Ka roller coaster, (which is located in New Jersey) is the fastest roller coaster in North America.
8. Noah Webster, (who authored the famous dictionary) attended Yale College.

Follow the directions for each item.

1. Write a complex sentence.

2. Write a sentence w*** ____

   Answers will vary.

3. Write a compound sentence.

66

Page 67

Capitalize the first word of **every sentence**.
   When they are attacked, honeybees release a chemical that smells like bananas.
Capitalize the first word in **direct quotations**.
   "Please remember to take out the garbage," said Mom.
Do not capitalize indirect quotations.
   The coach said that the game would not be canceled.

If a continuous sentence in a direct quotation is split and the second half is not a new sentence, do not capitalize it.
   "Pack your toothbrush," said Dad, "*and* at least one change of clothes."

If a new sentence begins after the split, then capitalize it as you would any sentence.
   "I think you'll feel better soon," said Dr. Raul. "*If* you don't, please call and leave a message with the front desk."

In a letter, capitalize the name of the street, the city, the state, and the month in the heading.
   1548 *Wishing Well Lane*
   Wichita, Kansas 67037
   June 5, 2014

Capitalize the salutation, or greeting, as well as the name of the person who is receiving the letter. Capitalize the first word of the closing.
   Dear Mr. Ball,   To whom it may concern: Your friend,   Sincerely,

Rewrite It
Rewrite each sentence below using correct capitalization.

1. "what time is your swim meet this week?" asked Mom.
   "What time is your swim meet this week?" asked Mom.
2. "it starts at 11:00," replied Paloma, "but the coach wants us there at 10:30."
   "It starts at 11:00," replied Paloma, "but the coach wants us there at 10:30."
3. "you need new goggles," said Mom. "the elastic on your old ones is wearing out."
   "You need new goggles," said Mom. "The elastic on your old ones is wearing out."
4. "let's wait until after the meet," said Paloma, "in case my goggles bring me good luck!"
   "Let's wait until after the meet," said Paloma, "in case my goggles bring me good luck!"

67

Page 68

Proof It
Proofread the following letter for mistakes in capitalization. Underline a lowercase letter three times to make it a capital. <u>m</u>

<u>o</u>ffice of community services
562 <u>w</u>est bank street
<u>s</u>pringvale, <u>v</u>ermont 05009

                                        <u>s</u>eptember 9, 2014

<u>d</u>ear Ms. <u>d</u>ominguez,
   <u>m</u>y family and I live in the Sardis Fields neighborhood, near the Beatty-Syms Creek. I enjoy riding my bike and hiking on the trails. <u>h</u>owever, in the last few weeks, I've been concerned by the amount of trash and litter I've noticed floating in the creek. <u>t</u>his is hazardous to the animals that make their homes in the area. It's also bad for the environment and unpleasant for all the people who bike, hike, and walk along the creek. <u>a</u>re there any groups who work to clean up the creek? <u>I</u>f there are, I'd be happy to help out. If there are not, I hope your office will consider starting a group. <u>p</u>lease help make cleaning up Beatty-Syms Creek a priority in our neighborhood!

<u>s</u>incerely,
Alysha Piazza

Try It
Write a dialogue between two or more people. Remember to follow the rules of capitalization.

Answers will vary.

68

Proper nouns are specific people, places, and things. Proper nouns are capitalized.
The class welcomed *Oscar* by giving a standing ovation. (specific person)
The mountains outside *Denver* glow beautifully during a sunset. (specific place)
My favorite brand of toothpaste is *Brite White*. (specific thing)

The titles of books, poems, songs, movies, plays, newspapers, and magazines are proper nouns and are capitalized. In a title, capitalize the first and last words, and capitalize all other words except *a, an,* and *the*. Do not capitalize short prepositions, such as *of, to, in, on,* and so on. Most titles are also underlined or set in italic font in text. Song titles, essays, poems, and other shorter works are placed in quotes.
The teacher read aloud a passage from *Little House on the Prairie*.
Randall played "Give Peace a Chance" on the saxophone.
An article about making cheese appeared in *Home Cooking Magazine*.
Last weekend, we saw the classic film *Miracle on 34th Street* at a theater.

Titles associated with names are also capitalized, but do not capitalize these titles if they are not directly used with the name.
Mayor Ed Koch served as *mayor* of New York City from 1978 to 1989.
Someday, Darrell hopes to become a *professor* as talented as *Professor*...

Find It

Write a complete ~~sentence to answer~~ the following questions. Be sure to capitalize any pro... ~~nouns~~ in your answers and format titles correctly.

Answers may vary. Possible answers:

1. What is the title of the last movie you saw?
The title of the last movie I saw was *Wreck-It Ralph*.

2. What city, state, or country would you like to visit most?
I would love to visit Stockholm, Sweden.

3. What is your favorite song or album?
My favorite album is The Beatles *Revolver*.

4. Who is the person you admire most?
I admire Dr. Martin Luther King Jr.

5. What book would you recommend for a friend to read?
I tell all my friends to read *The Watsons Go to Birmingham–1963*.

6. Where does the relative who lives farthest away from you live?
My Aunt Ida lives in Costa Rica.

69

Proof It
Correct the mistakes in capitalization using proofreading marks. Underline a lowercase letter three times to make it a capital. m̲

The idea that some land should be set aside for recreation began with president andrew jackson in 1832. He signed a law declaring that a hot spring in arkansas would be protected and available for use by the public. Thirty years later, abraham lincoln, who was president at the time, helped create the nation's first state park in yosemite valley, california. Eventually, the area would become yosemite national park, which is controlled by the united states government today. The honor of being the first national park, however, belongs to yellowstone national park. Located mostly in wyoming, with parts in in idaho and montana as well, yellowstone was established as a national park in march 1872 when president ulysses s. grant signed it into law.

During the next 40 years, several more national parks were established. Famous conservationist theodore roosevelt designated five more parks during his presidency. He also established the first four national monuments, which included devil's tower in wyoming. Today, 397 parks, monuments, and other sites are spread across the united states and are protected by the federal government. They even include the white house and the statue of liberty. If you want to learn more about national parks, watch ken burns's documentary *the national parks: america's best idea*.

Try It
Write a brief biography about yourself. Describe when and where you were born, who your parents or other relatives are, where your ancestors lived, where you go to school, and any other information you would like to include. Be sure to correctly capitalize proper nouns.

Answers will vary.

70

Organizations, departments of government, and sections of the country are all **proper nouns** and are capitalized.
The names of organizations, associations, and businesses are capitalized.
Carolina Waterfowl Rescue   The Rotary Club   Nike, Inc.
Capitalize the names of departments of government.
Department of Education   Department of Homeland Security
Directional words that point out particular sections of the country are capitalized. However, words that give directions are not capitalized.
The *West Coast* is experiencing a drought this summer.
The ranch is located *west* of the Rockies.

Historical events, nationalities, and team names are proper nouns, as well.
Events, periods of time, and important documents from history are capitalized.
Abigail studied the *Civil War* while in college.
Names of languages and nationalities are capitalized. They are also capitalized when they are used as adjectives.
Raul and Donita Jiminez won the *Latin* dance competition.
The names of sports teams are capitalized.
LeBron James left the *Cleveland Cavaliers* to play for the *Miami Heat*.

Solve It
Write a complete sentence to answer each of the following questions. Be sure to capitalize any proper nouns in your answers and to format titles correctly.

What name did Mark Twain and Charles Dudley Warner coin to describe the era in the United States spanning 1875 to 1900?

The G̲ I̲ L̲ D̲ E̲ D̲ A̲ G̲ E̲
     8 11 9 5 13 1 2

1. My grandfather worked at G̲eneral E̲lectric C̲ompany for nearly 40 years.

2. The D̲epartment of D̲efense coordinates and supervises national security.

3. We evacuated our beach house when a hurricane threatened the E̲ast C̲oast.

4. Quinton baked a G̲erman chocolate cake to bring to the potluck.

5. The L̲ions C̲lub members rode small motorcycles in the parade.

6. The I̲ndianapolis C̲olts play in the league championship this year.

7. Ideas from the A̲ge of E̲nlightenment influenced the writing of the D̲eclaration of I̲ndependence.

71

Complete It
Complete each sent... ~~sentence~~ ... or sentences that require a specific proper noun, it... ~~answer you want, but be sure you write a~~ proper noun that fits the description and that you capitalize your answer correctly.

Answers may vary. Possible answers:

1. I would love to see the **New York Knicks** (sports team) play the **Miami Heat** (sports team).

2. The United States entered **World War II** (name of a war) after Japan attacked Pearl Harbor.

3. **Pepperdine** (name of a college) is the best school in the **West** (directional word).

4. The **Bill of Rights** (historical document) guarantees certain freedoms for U.S. citizens.

5. During the **Civil War** (name of a war), Abraham Lincoln gave his famous **Gettysburg Address** (historical speech).

6. I already know how to speak **French** (language), but someday I would love to learn **Spanish** (language).

7. The U.S. **Supreme Court** (branch of the federal government) consists of nine judges.

8. The **Middle Ages** (historical period) in Europe are best known as the time of knights, peasants, and nobles.

9. The **Winter Olympics** (sporting event) feature events like figure skating and ski jumping.

10. Julia Child is famous for introducing **French** (nationality) cooking to Americans.

11. **Apple** (company name) first introduced the iPod in 2001.

12. The **Stone Age** (historical period) describes the time in human history before metal tools.

13. Most of my ancestors are **Polish** (nationality), but I am also part **Cherokee** (nationality).

14. I am a member of **Webelos** (name of club), and someday would also like to be a member of **the Boy Scouts** (name of club).

15. Michael Jordan is best known for playing basketball with the **Chicago Bulls** (sports team).

72

Periods are used at the end of declarative sentences and some imperative sentences.
Lattice encloses the garden and keeps out rabbits and deer.
Put paper in this box and cans in the other box.
Question marks are used at the end of interrogative sentences.
Where is the magnetic North Pole located?
Who sent the flowers to Ms. Mickelson?
Exclamation points are used at the end of exclamatory sentences. They are also used at the end of imperative sentences that show urgency, strong surprise, or emotion.
Mia Hamm is coming to visit our school!
Look at that eagle!

Complete It
Add an end mark to each sentence below.

1. That car just about hit Phinn _._
2. Did you see the license plate _?_
3. The car was moving too fast to read the numbers _._
4. Hand me a pencil or pen, please _._
5. I'm going to write down the make and model of the car _._
6. Do you know what model year it was _?_
7. Here comes another car going too fast _!_
8. Slow down _!_
9. What can be done about all these speeders _?_
10. We should write to someone in the city government _._
11. That's a great idea _!_
12. Maybe the city could put a couple of speed bumps along this road _._
13. Would you help me write the letter _?_
14. Call me about it later tonight _._
15. I don't think I have your number _._
16. Write it down on that piece of paper _._
17. Hey, I just remembered something that could help us _!_
18. What is it _?_
19. My cousin is good friends with the mayor's assistant _._
20. Let's call him _!_

73

Identify It
Circle the end mark that correctly completes each sentence.

1. Hollywood, California, is known as the moviemaking capital of the Untied States (. ? !)
2. Have you ever heard of Bollywood (. ? !)
3. Bollywood is the moviemaking capital of the Indian film industry (. ? !)
4. Do you know why it is called Bollywood (. ? !)
5. The capital of India is Mumbai, but the city used to be called Bombay (. ? !)
6. Bollywood gets its *B* from Bombay (. ? !)
7. The Indian film industry releases nearly 1,000 movies each year (. ? !)
8. That's a lot of movies (. ? !)
9. What are *masala movies* (. ? !)
10. Masala is a mixture of spices used in Indian cooking (. ? !)
11. Bollywood films are known for mixing many different genres into the same movie (. ? !)
12. A movie will have comedy, drama, singing, dancing, and action sequences (. ? !)
13. Like spicy masala used for cooking, masala movies have many different ingredients (. ? !)
14. With that many ingredients, masala movies often last for three hours or more (. ? !)
15. I could never sit still so long (. ? !)
16. The actors and actresses show their emotions through singing and dancing (. ? !)
17. What would it be like in real life if everyone suddenly broke into song and began dancing (. ? !)
18. Imagine the fun (. ? !)

Try It
Write one example of each type of sentence listed below. Be sure to use the correct end mark.

Imperative sentence showing excitement or emotion: _____

Declarative sentence: _____ Answers will vary.
Interrogative sentence: _____
Imperative sentence: _____

74

Review: Capitalization of Sentences, Quotations, Names, Titles, Places, and Other Proper Nouns; End Marks

Proofread each sentence below for capitalization. Lowercase a letter by making a slash through it /M/, and capitalize a letter by making three lines below it m.

1. Kate grew up on the east coast, but after college, she moved to New Mexico.
2. "does the play start at 6 or 6:30?" asked Will. "If we leave now, we should be on time."
3. I just learned that uncle Gordon has worked for the department of health and human services for more than 20 years.
4. Vidas is lithuanian, although he doesn't speak the language.
5. Mr. Temple's first article appeared in *photography today* magazine.
6. When I visited her last summer, my aunt bought my favorite cereal—green earth granola.
7. To reach the wilton museum of arts and crafts, turn west on broad street.
8. Did you know that six presidents have been named James?
9. Donita plans to be a doctor someday, but she hasn't decided on a specialty yet.
10. "Did the water expand or contract," wondered Stuart, "after you put it in the freezer?"
11. Did you know that portuguese is the official language of brazil?
12. Ms. Malone said that if you read the materials, you shouldn't have any problems on the test.
13. Dad doesn't follow professional sports, but he's a big fan of the nebraska huskers.
14. Next year, the Khem family plans to visit grand teton national park in wyoming during summer vacation.
15. "Olivia, we just won two tickets to the Academy Awards!" shouted Mrs. Nagy.

75

Review: Capitalization of Letter Parts, End Marks

Read each letter part below. If it is correct, make a check mark on the line. If it contains an error in capitalization, make an **X** on the line.

1. ✓ Seattle, WA 98107
2. X Yours Truly,
3. X To Whom It May Concern:
4. X Mount vernon, OH 43050
5. X Dear davis,
6. ✓ Sincerely,
7. X august 14, 2014
8. X your friend,

Add the appropriate end mark to each sentence below.

1. Spring peepers, tiny frogs, fill their vocal sacs with air that makes a sound when it is released _._
2. Wow, a hailstone can weigh more than two pounds _!_
3. The presidential $1-coin program is similar to the state quarters program _._
4. Winter solstice, which is celebrated by people all over the world, is the shortest day of the year _._
5. Did you know that wildfires can create a tornado of fire called a fire whirl _?_
6. The first American circus debuted in 1793 _._
7. Mariah and her sister made a gingerbread house that weighs 22 pounds _!_
8. The existence of rogue waves, or freak waves, was thought to be a myth not long ago _._
9. Have you ever tried to make your own paints from natural materials _?_
10. Is it true that Harriet Tubman served as a Union spy during the Civil War _?_
11. Watch out for that dog _!_
12. Do you know when Chinese New Year falls this year _?_
13. Chop the vegetables, and then add them to the wok _._

76

Page 77

Series commas are used with three or more items listed in a sentence. The items can be words or phrases and are separated by commas.
The Nile, the Amazon, and the Yangtze are among the longest rivers in the world.
To make granola, we'll need oats, nuts, dried fruit, and honey.

Commas are used to separate the name of a person spoken to from the rest of the sentence. This is called a **direct address**.
Sato, where did you leave your backpack?
Thanks so much for coming, Mr. Claussen.

When **multiple adjectives** describe a noun, they are separated by commas.
I bought the fresh, sweet cherries at the farmers' market.
Audrey made some bright, colorful paintings for her bedroom.

Make sure the adjectives equally modify the noun. If they are coordinate adjectives, you can switch the order without changing the meaning.
The eager, impulsive child could not wait her turn. (coordinate adjectives)
Zane wore shiny rubber boots. (non-coordinate adjectives)

Read the sentences below. Add commas where they are needed. If the sentence is correct as it is, make a check mark on the line.

Proof It
1. _____ Owen, do you know how to make your own soft pretzels?
2. _____ You'll need warm water, yeast, sugar, flour, salt, butter, and an egg.
3. _____ The soft, warm pretzels will taste delicious.
4. ✓ Put the yeast in a bowl, add the water, and stir in the sugar.
5. ✓ Please preheat the oven to 425°, Kate.
6. _____ Put the dough in a bowl, cover it, and allow it to rise.
7. _____ Can you wash the measuring cup, wooden spoon, and bowl, Owen?
8. ✓ Roll out the dough, shape it, and place it on a baking sheet.
9. _____ The salty, chewy crust on the pretzels turned out perfectly.
10. ✓ A glass of nice, cold iced tea would taste wonderful with the pretzels.
11. _____ Kate, did you hear the timer go off?
12. _____ Grab the square red plate, and we'll take some pretzels to Louie, Jake, and Nadia.

77

Page 78

Match It
Read the sentences below. Decide what kind of comma (if any) is needed in each sentence. Write the letter of your answer on the line.

a. series comma   b. direct address comma
c. multiple adjectives comma   d. no comma needed

1. _c_ The library smelled of dusty, well-read old books.
2. _d_ Isaiah, do you want to go to the library after school?
3. _a_ Breyton likes to read mysteries, science fiction and biographies.
4. _b_ How long have you been a librarian, Ms. Nealy?
5. _d_ Many patrons like to read on the soft leather couches by the fireplace.
6. _d_ If you join the summer reading club, you have the opportunity to earn stickers, pencils, CDs, and books.
7. _d_ Sierra volunteers at the library on Mondays, Thursdays, and Saturdays.
8. _c_ That old crumbling building at the corner used to be the town library when my grandmother was a child.
9. _d_ The enormous dictionary has a decorative leather cover.
10. _d_ Teddy borrowed books about Brazil, the moon, and woodworking.

Try It
For each number below, write a sentence that includes the items in parentheses.

Answers may vary. Possible answers :

1. (series commas and direct address)
   Mr. Yang, will you please call Melissa, Thomas, and Henry?
2. (multiple adjectives)
   The rusty, creaking swings at the park will be replaced.
3. (multiple adjectives and direct address)
   Sammi, hand me that colorful, striped vase.
4. (series commas)
   We traveled to Russia, Ukraine, and Poland.
5. (direct address)
   Marcie, take the dog for a walk.

78

Page 79

NAME _____

Lesson 2.6 Commas: Combining Sentences, Setting Off Dialogue

Use a comma to **combine two independent clauses** with a coordinate conjunction.
The researcher opened the door to the cage, and a small, white mouse crawled into his hand.

In a complex sentence, **connect a dependent and an independent clause** with a comma and subordinate conjunction.
Because Jared's glasses had broken, he was unable to take the English test.

Commas are used when **setting off dialogue** from the rest of the sentence.
Aunt Helen replied, "I don't know if you're aware of what you're getting into!"
"If you want to watch a movie before bed," hollered Dad, "you'll have to get started right now!"

Identify It
Read each sentence below. If it is correct, write **C** on the line. If it is incorrect, write **X** on the line and add commas where they are needed.

1. _C_ India is a peninsula, which means it is surrounded by water on three sides.
2. _X_ Although part of India is desert, it also has jungles and mountains.
3. _X_ Cows are sacred in India, so Hindus do not eat beef.
4. _X_ Sean asked, "Did you know that the oldest Indian civilization began about 5,000 years ago?"
5. _X_ Mahatma Gandhi, a famous Indian pacifist, was instrumental in helping India gain independence from Britain.
6. _X_ "Our flight to New Delhi leaves at 8:00," began Nigel, "but I'd like to be at the airport at least two hours before that."
7. _C_ Because India has so many different climates, it is home to thousands of species of animals.
8. _C_ "We visited many relatives on our trip to India, but we also stopped at many tourist destinations," said Sanj.
9. _X_ By the mid 1750s, Britain controlled much of India.

79

Page 80

NAME _____

Lesson 2.6 Commas: Combining Sentences, Setting Off Dialogue

Proof It
Read the selection below. Add commas where they are needed using proofreaders' marks. Fifteen commas are missing.

Addy walked into the kitchen, where her mom was preparing a stir-fry for dinner.
"Mom, have you ever heard of Hurricane Hunters?" she asked.
Mrs. Hawthorne opened a carton of mushrooms, and she handed them to Addy to chop. "I think so," she responded. "I don't really know much about them, though."
"We watched a documentary about them in science today, and I think I want to be one!" exclaimed Addy, scraping the mushroom into the wok. "I've thought about joining the Air Force after high school, and I love science. I think it would be a perfect career for me."
"Tell me more about them," said Mrs. Hawthorne. "I'm not sure exactly what Hurricane Hunters do."
Addy stirred the vegetables. "Hurricane Hunters fly right into the eye of a hurricane, where they gather data about the storm. They measure wind speed, and they look for the pressure center. The data they send back can help forecasters do their job."
"It sounds so interesting, Addy," said her mom, "but it also sounds incredibly dangerous."
Addy smiled and replied, "I knew you'd say that, so I'm prepared. Although it is a dangerous job, they've flown over 100,000 hours without a problem!"
"Oh, Addy," sighed Mrs. Hawthorne, "you've always been a daredevil."

Try It
Write a short dialogue between yourself and a family member. Remember to use commas correctly in your writing.

_____

_____

Answers will vary.

_____

_____

_____

80

Page 81

Commas are used in both **personal** and **business letters**.

Personal Letters
Commas appear in four of the five parts of the personal letter.

Heading: 15228 River Rock Ave.
Santa Fe, NM 87004
February 27, 2014
Salutation: Dear Pilar,
Body: comma usage in sentences
Closing: Yours truly,

Business Letters
Commas appear in four of the six parts of the business letter.

Heading: 601 Dillingham Ct.
St. Paul, MN 55108
July 18, 2014
Inside Address: Dr. Clare Yoshida
Four Oaks Medical Center
1189 Hampton Rd.
Hartford, CT 06103
Body: comma usage in sentences
Closing: Sincerely,

Rewrite It
Rewrite each item below. Include commas where they are needed.

1. Your friend Your friend,
2. April 14 1809 April 14, 1809
3. My degree is in marketing and I have had several internships.
   My degree is in marketing, and I have had several internships.
4. Regards Regards,
5. San Rafael CA 94903 San Rafael, CA 94903
6. We visited the botanical gardens the planetarium and the art museum.
   We visited the botanical gardens, the planetarium, and the art museum.
7. Dear Grandma Suzanne Dear Grandma Suzanne,
8. All my best All my best,
9. August 11 2014 August 11, 2014
10. Rock Hill SC 29732 Rock Hill, SC 29732

Page 82

Proof It
Read the letter below and look for places where commas are missing. Use proofreaders' marks ^ to add the missing commas.

557 West Mound St.
Madison, WI 53532
October 21, 2014

Mr. George Cohen
Oakvale Public Library
1862 Lincoln Ln.
Madison, WI 53532

Dear Mr. Cohen:

My name is Elizabeth Yang, and I'm a seventh grade student at Roosevelt Middle School. I'm interested in becoming a volunteer at Oakvale Library. I know that many of your volunteers reshelve books. I would enjoy shelving books, but I'm also interested in working in the children's section. Perhaps I could help the children's librarian with story time? I love spending time with children, and I attended story time myself until I started elementary school. I have worked as a mother's helper for the last two summers, so I have quite a bit of experience working with young children. I have been an avid reader since I was five. I still remember many of my favorite books from that time!

I would be available on Wednesdays after school and on Sunday afternoons. I look forward to speaking with you about volunteer opportunities at the library. Thank you for your time and consideration.

Sincerely,
Elizabeth A. Yang
Elizabeth A. Yang

Try It
Write a letter to a friend or family member. Remember to use commas where needed, including in the body of the letter.

Answers will vary.

Page 83

Colons have several functions in a sentence.
Colons are used to introduce a series in a sentence. Colons are not needed when the series is preceded by a verb or preposition.
The Massey Glee Club performed in the following cities: *Roanoke, Danville,* and *Blacksburg.*
The flavors offered at the ice cream shop are chocolate, vanilla, and strawberry. (no colon needed)
Colons are sometimes used instead of a comma to set off a clause.
Maestro Bing told the orchestra: *"The third movement must be flawless."*
Colons are used to set off a word or phrase for emphasis.
Shawn's knees shook as he realized who was at the door: *Principal Nelson.*
Colons are used when writing the time.
We need to be waiting outside the station by *10:00.*
Business letters use colons in the salutation. *Dear Sir or Madam:*

A **semicolon** is a cross between a period and a comma.
Semicolons join two independent clauses when a coordinate conjunction is not used.
Bats are hibernating in the vents of my attic; they will need to be relocated in the spring.
Semicolons are used to separate clauses when they already contain commas.
Late at night, I heard cars honking, people yelling, and sirens blaring; which is why I cannot sleep.
Semicolons are also used to separate series of words or phrases that already contain commas.
Students in Mr. Hirochi's class measured, marked, and cut the cloth into pieces; sewed the pieces together in a pattern; and then displayed the finished quilt on the front wall.

Rewrite It
Rewrite the following sentences, adding colons or semicolons where needed.
1. Snow fell throughout the night by morning, the drifts were two feet high.
   Snow fell throughout the night; by morning, the drifts were two feet high.
2. Please pick up the following items at the store a hairbrush, toothpaste, three bars of soap, and a bottle of lotion.
   Please pick up the following items at the store: a hairbrush, toothpaste, three bars of soap, and a bottle of lotion.
3. This morning I downloaded apps for my MP3 player, phone, and tablet I walked the dog to the park and back and I cleaned out my car.
   This morning I downloaded apps for my MP3 player, phone, and tablet; I walked the dog to the park and back; and I cleaned out my car.
4. At the post office this morning, you won't believe who I saw Jude Law.
   At the post office this morning, you won't believe who I saw: Jude Law.

Page 84

Proof It
In the sentences below, colons and semicolons are missing or used incorrectly. Correct each sentence by adding, replacing, or deleting colons and semicolons as needed.

1. The string quartet consists of: a cello, a viola, and two violins.
2. The two violinists practice together every other day; they are determined to make no mistakes at the concert.
3. The cellist, Henry Warner, gets up very early to practice each morning: 4:00 A.M.!
4. At the last concert, right in the middle of a song, a string broke on Helen's viola; but as she replaced it, the audience waited patiently.
5. At each performance, Helen wears a black dress, high heels, and a lucky brooch; she wishes her fellow musicians a good show; and she calls her mother afterward.
6. These venues will host their next three concerts: Royal Music Hall, Lakeside Auditorium, and the Bentley Music Center.
7. Cellos are bigger than violins; they also produce a deeper sound.
8. Henry reminded Helen, "Make sure you have new strings on your viola."
9. The concert at the Royal Music Hall is scheduled to begin at 7:30.
10. The first violist to join the quartet was Janice Stringer; Molly Hills joined second.
11. The quartet will play pieces by: Beethoven, Mozart, and Brahms.
12. Although the Beethoven piece is rather difficult, Helen had played it before; so when the quartet first practiced it, she helped teach the others.
13. The quartet decided to include one piece as a surprise for the audience: Bob Dylan's "All Along the Watchtower."
14. Three special guests attended the performance: Mayor Hank Satterly, Professor Mia Ling, and the well-known cellist Yo-Yo Ma.
15. The quartet strode onstage; the audience erupted with applause.
16. After the players sat down, they took a moment to tune their instruments; and then after a brief pause, they launched into the first song.
17. The four bows swept across, jumped over, and sawed against the strings; the music filled the concert hall; and the audience basked in the beauty.
18. Mingled with the applause that followed, one word rang out from different parts of the hall: "Bravo!"

85

Quotation marks are used to show the exact words of a speaker. The quotation marks are placed before and after the exact words.

"Did you bring flowers for Alice?" asked Carl. "Her party starts in about an hour."

Quotation marks are also used when a direct quotation contains another direct quotation.

Hector explained, "Beth said, 'Take the train, or you'll get stuck in traffic.'"

Note that single quotation marks are used to set off the inside quotation. Single quotes express what Beth said. Double quotes express what Hector said.

Quotation marks are used with some titles. Quotation marks are used with the titles of short stories, poems, songs, and articles in magazines and newspapers.

My favorite poem in A. A. Milne's *When We Were Very Young* is "At the Zoo."

If a title is quoted within a direct quotation, then single quotation marks are used.

Melinda asked, "Have you read 'Flight' by John Steinbeck?"

Complete It
Add double or single quotation marks where they are needed in each sentence.

1. "We need to determine how many ducks arrived at the pond yesterday," Dr. Steinberg explained.

2. Lotta reassured the others when she said, "Mr. Yates said, 'Don't worry if the experiment fails the first time.' So we just need to try again."

3. "My favorite song of all time is 'Yellow Submarine' by The Beatles," said Laura.

4. "We should probably get going," said Dawna. "The doctor said, 'Arrive fifteen minutes early to fill out some paperwork before your exam.'"

5. "Our neighbors, the Worths, are installing a pool," said Mia.

6. After his sister recited some of "The Rime of the Ancient Mariner," Noah asked, "You don't have to memorize the whole poem do you?"

7. "The title of my essay is 'What's Next for Staunton?'" the mayor explained.

8. "How much money did you bring?" Jessie asked. "The tickets are almost $20 apiece."

9. Before Katie left on the trip, she read an article entitled "Don't Get Lost: Ten Tips for Using a Compass."

10. As Lucas studied the image, he remembered what his teacher had said. "A skull is usually a symbol for mortality."

86

Proof It
The passage below contains several errors with quotation marks. Edit the passage to correct the mistakes.

Ms. Langstrom said, "For the next couple of weeks, we will be reading short stories and poems by author and poet Gary Soto." "Has anyone read his work before?"

Katie raised her hand and replied, "Last year at my old school, we read most of *Baseball in April and Other Stories*. My favorite story was 'La Bamba.'"

"Today, I will read the poem 'Ode to Family Photographs,'" Ms. Langstrom explained.

As she read aloud, Luis whispered to Katie, "One time my dad said, 'Poems are like X-rays of the world.' I've always remembered that."

Luis looked up. Ms. Langstrom had stopped reading and was staring at him. "Do you have something to share with us, Luis?"

"I'm sorry, Ms. Langstrom. I was telling Katie something my dad once said. He described poems as being "like X-rays of the world."

"That's a nice simile, Luis," Ms. Langstrom agreed, "but I wish you'd wait until I'm done reading to talk about it."

"Yes, Ma'am," replied Luis.

Ms. Langstrom finished the reading. Then, she asked the students to name other poems they knew.

"'I Wandered Lonely as a Cloud' is the only poem I can name," admitted Kieran.

"That's the famous first line of Wordsworth's 'Daffodils,' Kieran," Ms. Langstrom clarified. "But it's not the title."

The teacher began handing out copies of *Baseball in April*. "Everybody, please read the story 'Broken Chain' by Wednesday." Then, she smiled at Katie and added, "This should mostly be a review for you, Katie, so I expect good work."

Try It
Write a short dialogue between two friends discussing their favorite songs. Be sure to use single and double quotes where they are needed.

Answers will vary.

87

When you are working on a computer, use **italics** for the titles of books, plays, movies, television series, magazines, and newspapers. If you are writing by hand, **underline** these titles.

Pride and Prejudice is my favorite book, as well as my mother's. (book)
Maxwell's parents have a subscription to *The New York Times*. (newspaper)
Serena loves to watch the show *Bizarre Foods* with her brothers. (TV show)

Identify It
Underline the title or titles in each sentence that should be italicized.

1. Micah enjoys learning about science and nature, so his grandpa got him a subscription to <u>Odyssey</u> magazine.

2. <u>The Boy Who Dared</u> is a fictional book about World War II and Hitler's rise to power.

3. Everyone in my family enjoys watching the show <u>Modern Family</u>.

4. Tiana and her parents are going to see a production of Shakespeare's <u>A Midsummer Night's Dream</u> at a park downtown.

5. Eli is writing a research paper about Ruby Bridges, so he borrowed the book <u>Through My Eyes</u> from the library.

6. Julia loved the movie <u>Little Women</u> as much as she loved the book.

7. Have you read <u>Does My Head Look Big in This</u> by Randa Abdel-Fattah?

8. If you like adventure stories, you must read the book <u>Raft</u> by Stephanie Bodeen.

9. I need to find the article about the current bee crisis that was in last Sunday's <u>Washington Post</u>.

10. My school is going to be putting on the play <u>Alice</u>, which is based on Lewis Carroll's famous book, <u>Alice's Adventures in Wonderland</u>.

11. On Saturday, Jian went to the 3:00 showing of <u>The Watsons Go to Birmingham</u>.

12. Carrie's photo was in the Arts section of the <u>Kansas City Star</u>.

13. The school library has hundreds of copies of <u>National Geographic</u>.

14. My favorite episode of <u>Survivorman</u> takes place in the Arctic.

88

Try It
Answer each of the following questions with c[...]

Answers may vary.
Possible answers:

1. What book have you read recently that you would recommend to a friend?
<u>I would recommend Fantastic Mr. Fox.</u>

2. What is the name of a movie you've seen that that is based on a book?
<u>Last week, I saw Charlotte's Web.</u>

3. What magazine have you used as a source for a school paper or essay?
<u>For my report about frogs, I used an article from Kids Discover.</u>

4. If you could go to New York City and see a play performed on Broadway, what would it be?
<u>I would see The Pirates of Penzance.</u>

5. What is the title of a book you've read (or would like to read) more than once?
<u>I've read How to Eat Fried Words about six times.</u>

6. What is the name of your hometown newspaper?
<u>My family subscribes to The Lincoln Journal-Star.</u>

7. If you could get a free subscription to a magazine, which magazine would it be?
<u>I would choose New Moon Girls.</u>

8. What television show would you recommend to your best friend?
<u>I tell everyone to watch The Jeff Corwin Experience.</u>

9. What was your favorite movie when you were in first grade?
<u>I loved Shrek.</u>

10. Have you ever quit reading or watching in the middle of a book or a movie? What was it called?
<u>Yes, I really did not like Little House on the Prairie, and I quit reading after just a couple of chapters.</u>

Page 89

Apostrophes are used in contractions, to form possessives, and to form plurals. Apostrophes take the place of the omitted letters in contractions.
we will = we'll   would not = wouldn't

Possessives show possession, or ownership. To form the possessive of a singular noun, add an apostrophe and an s. This rule applies even if the noun already ends in s.
The koala's fur was thick and soft.   Is that Charles's car?

To form the possessive of plural nouns ending in s, add an apostrophe. If the plural noun does not end in s, add both the apostrophe and an s.
The chefs' opinions about the new restaurant appear in the review.
The children's boots are lined up by the door.

Identify It
Read each sentence below. If the apostrophes are used correctly, make a check mark on the line. If they are used incorrectly or are missing, make an **X** on the line.

1. ✓ Karim's yoga class meets at 4:00 on Wednesday afternoon.
2. X The girls running club was started by Missy Polaski and Anya Padma.
3. X As the buzzer rang, we could hear the parents cheers echoing through the stadium.
4. X Serenity should'nt miss volleyball practice again this week.
5. X Mattys' hiking club is planning to walk a section of the Appalachian Trail this weekend.
6. ✓ The year-end party for the lacrosse team is going to be held at the Baxters' house.
7. X Reggie cant play baseball again until his ankle is fully healed.
8. ✓ In spite of the students' cheers, Liam was able to focus on the ball and make a final goal.
9. X Although the coachs' voice was calm, we could tell how excited he was.
10. ✓ After an especially long swim practice, Selena's eyes were burning.
11. X Camerons' skis and poles were stolen last week!
12. ✓ We'll pick you up after your track meet.
13. X The Yellowjackets scored as a result of the quarterbacks' great throw.
14. ✓ Holly and Noah won't admit that the loss wasn't their fault.
15. X The Lakeshore Womens' Rowing Club is sponsoring the school's rowing team this year.

89

Page 90

Proof It
Each sentence below is missing at least one apostrophe. Add the apostrophes where they are needed using this proofreading mark ⌄ .

1. Cows⌄ manure is used as fertilizer on farms all across America.
2. What you probably didn't know, though, is that manure can be used to create power.
3. A single cow can produce about 30 gallons of manure a day—it's easy to see how much an entire dairy farm could produce!
4. Scientists⌄ solution for dealing with all that manure is to turn it into power.
5. A giant scooper cleans a barns⌄ floor of manure.
6. The manures⌄ placed in a giant tank called a digester.
7. The digesters⌄ job is similar to the job that occurs in a cows⌄ stomach.
8. If a farmers⌄ crops don't do well one year, it's nice to have another source of income.
9. Another benefit of cow manure energy is that it isn't a fossil fuel.
10. The USDAs⌄ Rural Energy for America program provides grants to Iowas⌄ farmers.
11. Utility companies need to be willing to buy farmers⌄ manure energy.
12. Liquid that is a byproduct of the digester is used as fertilizer and surprisingly doesn't smell at all!

Try It
On the lines below, write two sentences that include contractions and two that include possessives.

Answers will vary.

90

Page 91

Hyphens are used to divide words that come at the end of a line. Divide words between syllables.
Bradford Landscaping lined our driveway with monkey grasses and orna-mental flowering plants.
Do not divide one letter from the rest of the word, and divide syllables after the vowel if the vowel is a syllable by itself. Divide words with double consonants between the consonants.
associa-tion, not a-ssociation or associ-ation
hum-ming   mid-dle
Hyphens are used between compound numbers from twenty-one through ninety-nine.
Only twenty-seven of the class's thirty-one students attended the science fair.
Hyphens are used in compound modifiers only when the modifier precedes the word it modifies. Hyphens are not used for compound modifiers that include adverbs ending in -ly.
I presented a well-researched report to the board. My report was well researched.
Even a carefully built sandcastle will collapse eventually.
Use hyphens in some compound nouns. You will need to check in a dictionary to be sure which compound nouns need hyphens.
Mari and Lexi stood in line for a ride on the merry-go-round.
Dashes indicate a sudden break or a change in thought.
We took our rabbit—her name is Lily—outside to run around in the backyard.
Parentheses show supplementary, or additional, material or set off phrases in a stronger way than commas.
On the second Wednesday of next month (March 12) we will host a formal tea party.
Sunlight coming in the windows (the windows at the front of the house) has faded one side of our couch.

Complete It
Add hyphens where they are needed in the following sentences. Use a dictionary if you need help.

1. My mother-in-law, Mildred, is a self-taught artist.
2. She has twenty-five beautifully painted landscapes that are all well-protected inside a leather portfolio.
3. Her first-born child is my wife, Nancy.
4. Mildred thought painting was a long-lost skill, but she was pleasantly surprised to discover she was still a highly talented artist.
5. Recently, she had a well-attended exhibition at a locally owned gallery.

91

Page 92

Rewrite It
Rewrite the following sentences, adding parentheses, dashes, and hyphens where needed.

1. My great aunt visits us every Sunday even if there's a blizzard so we can cook together.
My great aunt visits us every Sunday—even if there's a blizzard—so we can cook together.
2. We use a well worn cookbook it was originally my great great grandmother's that contains about fifty five different recipes.
We use a well-worn cookbook (it was originally my great great grandmother's) that contains about fifty-five different recipes.
3. During the below freezing days of winter, we prefer cooking a belly warming pot of stew or soup.
During the below-freezing days of winter, we prefer cooking a belly-warming pot of stew or soup.
4. My not so patient younger brother his name is Eli mills around while we cook, trying to snatch samples what a pest!
My not-so-patient younger brother (his name is Eli) mills around while we cook, trying to snatch samples—what a pest!
5. Chopping onions is an eye stinging chore my eyes water and my nose runs, but I don't mind doing it.
Chopping onions is an eye-stinging chore—my eyes water and my nose runs, but I don't mind doing it.
6. Great Aunt Ruth handles the dangerously hot boiling broth we use organic chicken broth.
Great Aunt Ruth handles the dangerously hot boiling broth (we use organic chicken broth).
7. In summer, we cook with farm fresh vegetables bought at the farmer's market Saturday is market day.
In summer, we cook with farm-fresh vegetables bought at the farmer's market (Saturday is market day).
8. During the winter, our well stocked grocery store it's just a few blocks from our house provides the ingredients we need.
During the winter, our well-stocked grocery store (it's just a few blocks from our house) provides the ingredients we need.

Try It
Write three sentences below: one with a hyphen, one with a dash, and one with parentheses.
1.
2. Answers will vary.
3.

92

Answer Key

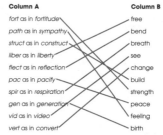

Page 97

Prefixes and suffixes change the meanings of root and base words. A **prefix** is a word part added to the beginning of a root or base word. For example, the prefix un- means "not" or "opposite," so unequal means "**not** equal."

Some common prefixes and their meanings are listed below.
in-, im-, ir-, il- = "not"	irregular, impolite
re- = "again"	refreeze
dis- = "not, opposite of"	disconnect
non- = "not"	nonslip
over- = "too much"	overcook
mis- = "wrongly"	miscalculate
pre- = "before"	precut
inter- = "between, among"	intercoastal

Match It
Write a word in the blank that matches each definition below. The word should contain a prefix and a base word found in the definition.

1. not cooked — uncooked
2. to understand wrongly — misunderstand
3. appear again — reappear
4. not visible — invisible
5. load too much — overload
6. discover again — rediscover
7. to diagnose wrongly — misdiagnose
8. not married — unmarried
9. to qualify before — prequalify
10. not mature — immature
11. the opposite of approve — disapprove
12. not living — nonliving
13. slept too much — overslept
14. between states — interstate

Page 98

A **suffix** is a word part added to the end of a root or base word. Sometimes, the spelling of the root or base word changes when a suffix is added. For example, the suffix -ness means "state or condition of." Happiness means "the state or condition of being happy." Note that the final -y in happy changes to i before adding the suffix.

Some common suffixes and their meanings are listed below.
-ful = "characterized by or tending to"	playful
-y = "characteristic of"	angrily
-er, -or = "one who" or "person connected with"	dreamer
-on, -tion, -ation, -ition = "act or process"	animation
-ic = "having characteristics of"	allergic
-less = "without"	harmless
-en = "made of" or "to make"	brighten

Solve It
Read each definition below. Fill in the correct space in the crossword puzzle with a word that ends in a suffix and matches the definition.

Across
1. without pain
4. act or process of competing
6. to make dark
7. characterized by beauty
9. to make thick
10. characterized by joy

Down
2. the state or condition of being shy
3. having characteristics of science
5. act or process of investigating
8. characteristic of history

Crossword answers: 1. painless, 4. competition, 7. darken, beautiful, 9. thicken, 10. joyful

Page 99

Complete It
Complete each sentence ~~Answers may vary. Possible answers:~~ for the word shown in italics. Use the root of the word ~~...~~ you can. Then, underline the word's prefix or suffix. Use ~~...ary if you need help.~~

1. Someone who is disloyal is <u>not loyal</u>
2. A surveyor is <u>someone who surveys</u>
3. If you predict an event that happens, you <u>tell about it before it happens</u>
4. I overestimated the cost of the meal, meaning I <u>expected the cost to be</u> over, or more than, the amount it turned out to be
5. To transfer money from a savings account to a checking account means <u>to move the money from</u> one account to the other
6. A worthy opponent is an opponent who <u>is worth competing against</u>
7. A building under construction is <u>still in the state of being constructed</u>
8. If you are flexible, then you <u>are able to flex</u>
9. An incorrect answer on a quiz is <u>an answer that is not correct</u>
10. Cooks often prefer nonstick pans because <u>food does not stick to them</u> when it is cooked

Try It
On each line below, write a sentence that includes a word with the prefix or suffix indicated.
1. the suffix -ful
2. the prefix un-
3. the prefix re-
4. the suffix -er ~~Answers will vary.~~
5. the prefix dis-
6. the prefix pre-

Page 100

Identify It
Identify twelve words in the passage below that contain a prefix, a suffix, or both a prefix and a suffix. Use the lines below to identify the different words parts. Some words may have more than one suffix. One example has been provided.

A rat quickly scurries across the jungle floor. Nearby, a predator lies patiently in the dense underbrush, soundless and still. Suddenly, more than 10 feet of solid muscular power launches at the rat, and in an instant, the rat is in the attacker's mouth. This predator is a boa constrictor, but it isn't ready to eat yet. These snakes are not venomous—their bites are not deadly—and swallowing the animal alive would be foolish and harmful. A live rat would scratch and bite the snake's insides. Instead, the boa uses its powerful body to squeeze the rat and restrict airflow into its lungs. Soon, respiration ceases, and the boa can swallow its prey safely. Boas have stretchy tissue connecting their jaws, so they can open their jaws extremely wide, enabling them to swallow ~~...~~ rat, like all of the boa's prey, is swallowed whole. Dig ~~Answers may vary. Possible answers:~~ way through the snake's body. After consuming a s ~~...~~ ght not require additional food for several weeks. Sat ~~...~~ with its fat snack, this boa is ready to retire for the evening.

	Prefix	Root	Suffix
1.	con	strict	or
2.		quick	ly
3.		predat	or
4.	under	brush	
5.		venom	ous
6.	re	strict	
7.	re	spir	ation
8.	con	nect	ing
9.	en	abl	ing
10.		diges	tion
11.	re	quire	
12.		addi	tional

Try It
Using the root word form, add prefixes and suffixes to create new words. How many different words can you create? Write them on the lines below.
formed, forming, formation, information, reform, conform, reformed, deform, formula, informed, informing, reformed, conforming, transform, transformed, unformed, perform

Double negatives occur when two negative words are used in the same sentence. Negative words include *not, no, never, nobody, nowhere, nothing, barely, hardly, scarcely,* and contractions containing the word *not.* Avoid using double negatives—they are grammatically incorrect.

To correct a double negative, you can delete one of the negative words or replace it with an affirmative, or positive, word. Affirmative words are the opposite of negative words. Examples include *some, somewhere, someone, anyone, any,* and *always.*

 Negative: Mr. Zingale *can't* do anything until Ava's parents arrive.
 Double Negative: Mr. Zingale *can't* do *nothing* until Ava's parents arrive.

 Negative: *Don't* use any slang in your e-mail to Ms. Sanchez.
 Double Negative: *Don't* use *no* slang in your e-mail to Ms. Sanchez.

Complete It
Underline the word or words in parentheses that best complete each sentence below.

1. Because of the icy runway, the airplane couldn't go (nowhere, <u>anywhere</u>).
2. Sullivan doesn't think that that (nobody, <u>anyone</u>) is going to come to his play because of the storm.
3. We hoped to receive extra credit for the handout we made for our presentation, but we didn't get (<u>any</u>, none).
4. Aunt Kat could barely see (<u>anything</u>, nothing) through the heavy downpour.
5. Isis won't (<u>ever</u>, never) finish his book report unless he gets some quiet time to work.
6. Lauren does not have (no, <u>any</u>) air in her bike tires.
7. Our ancient tabby cat, Miss Pibbles, hardly (never, <u>ever</u>) eats all her canned food.
8. Carson (<u>can</u>, can't) never contain his excitement when they arrive at the beach.
9. Although he was here for two hours, the plumber didn't do (nothing, <u>anything</u>) about the leak under the kitchen sink.
10. Deepak hardly missed (<u>any</u>, no) classes this semester.
11. Nobody (<u>can</u>, can't) grow juicy, red tomatoes better than my dad.
12. Julian drove around for 15 minutes, but couldn't find (nowhere, <u>anywhere</u>) to park.
13. The police officer won't have (no, <u>any</u>) back-up until her partner arrives at 9:00.
14. The bear and her cub scarcely (<u>ever</u>, never) come into town in the summer.

101

Rewrite It
Each sentence below contains a double negative. Rewrite the sentences to eliminate the double negatives. There may be more than one correct answer for each item.

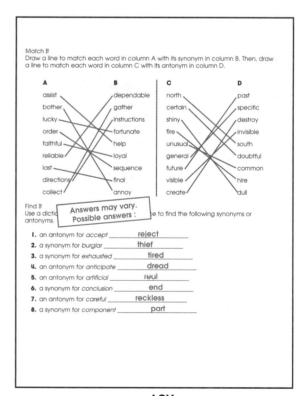

1. The birds wouldn't eat none of the new birdseed.
 The birds wouldn't eat any of the new birdseed.
2. Don't nobody touch the wet paint on the fence!
 Nobody touch the wet paint on the fence!
3. Ian was sleeping so deeply that he didn't hardly hear the fire alarm go off.
 Ian was sleeping so deeply that he didn't hear the fire alarm go off.
4. The swim team wasn't interested in nothing but practicing the day before the meet.
 The swim team wasn't interested in anything but practicing the day before the meet.
5. The Girl Scouts are not going nowhere this weekend.
 The Girl Scouts are not going anywhere this weekend.
6. Nobody can't join the club without a unanimous vote.
 Nobody can join the club without a unanimous vote.
7. Madison hasn't never traveled outside of the United States.
 Madison has never traveled outside of the United States.
8. The Johannsens didn't remember to do nothing about the broken gate.
 The Johannsens didn't remember to do anything about the broken gate.

Try It
Write three sentences using double negatives.

1. _____
2. _____
   Answers will vary.
3. _____

102

Synonyms are words that have the same, or almost the same, meaning. Using synonyms can help you avoid repeating words and can make your writing more interesting. A thesaurus, either in book form or online, is a good source for finding synonyms.
 trash/garbage   accomplish/achieve   raise/ lift   empty/vacant

Antonyms are words that have opposite meanings. A dictionary, either in book form or online, is a good source for finding antonyms.
 attract/repel   accept/decline   common/rare

Rewrite It
Rewrite each sentence [Answers may vary. Possible answers :] synonym for **boldface** words and an antonym for underlined words.

1. Is that a **genuine** piece of turquoise?
 Is that a real piece of turquoise?
2. There is no doubt in my mind that the defendant is <u>guilty</u>.
 There is no doubt in my mind that the defendant is innocent.
3. It wouldn't be <u>difficult</u> for me to read the text if you could **magnify** it.
 It would be easy for me to read the text if you could enlarge it.
4. The security guard **examined** the bags before she **allowed** the couple through the gates.
 The security guard searched the bags before she let the couple through the gates.
5. What kind of **occupation** are you <u>interested</u> in pursuing?
 What kind of job are you uninterested in pursuing?
6. Although I have **searched**, I cannot find a <u>solution</u>.
 Although I have looked, I cannot find a problem.
7. This year, David hopes to <u>decrease</u> the amount of sugar he **consumes**.
 This year, David hopes to increase the amount of sugar he eats.
8. We need to stake the sapling so that its trunk will **remain** <u>straight</u>.
 We need to stake the sapling so that its trunk will stay bent.
9. Will the Coast Guard be able to **rescue** the passengers on the boat?
 Will the Coast Guard be able to save the passengers on the boat?

103

Match It
Draw a line to match each word in column A with its synonym in column B. Then, draw a line to match each word in column C with its antonym in column D.

A	B	C	D
assist	dependable	north	past
bother	gather	certain	specific
lucky	instructions	shiny	destroy
order	fortunate	fire	invisible
faithful	help	unusual	south
reliable	loyal	general	doubtful
last	sequence	future	common
directions	final	visible	hire
collect	annoy	create	dull

Find It
Use a dicti[Answers may vary. Possible answers :] e to find the following synonyms or antonyms.

1. an antonym for *accept*   reject
2. a synonym for *burglar*   thief
3. a synonym for *exhausted*   tired
4. an antonym for *anticipate*   dread
5. an antonym for *artificial*   real
6. a synonym for *conclusion*   end
7. an antonym for *careful*   reckless
8. a synonym for *component*   part

104

105

An **analogy** is a comparison between two pairs of words. To complete an analogy, figure out how the pairs of words are related.
Forest is to *tree* as *beach* is to *sand.*
A forest consists of trees, just as a beach consists of sand.

Leap is to *jump* as *soar* is to *fly.*
Leap is a synonym for jump, just as soar is a synonym for fly.

Lens is to *camera* as *page* is to *book.*
A lens is a part of a camera, just as a page is part of a book.

Analogies are often presented without using the phrase *is to* and the word *as.* Instead, colons are used in place of *is to,* and two colons are used in place of *as* to separate the pairs being compared.
Movie is to *DVD* as *album* is to *CD.*
movie : DVD :: album : CD

Complete It
Circle the letter of the word that best completes each analogy.

1. ice : water :: candle : _____
   a. light   b. fire   (c.) wax   d. heat
2. tree : bark :: fish : _____
   a. ocean   (b.) scales   c. water   d. fin
3. _____ : canoe :: bus : bicycle
   a. rowboat   b. kayak   c. speedboat   (d.) ocean liner
4. recipe : cooking :: _____ : traveling
   (a.) map   b. tickets   c. airplane   d. restaurant
5. form : information :: act : _____
   a. directions   (b.) inaction   c. technology   d. play
6. paper : scissors :: rock : _____
   (a.) chisel   b. sharp   c. solid   d. gravel
7. mountain : _____ :: exterior : interior
   a. cliff   b. peak   c. ocean   (d.) valley
8. _____ : blades :: car : wheel
   a. knife   (b.) fan   c. wind   d. electricity

106

Solve It
To solve each analogy below, unscramble the word in parentheses and write it on the line.

1. *Rays* are to *sun* as ___petals___ are to *flower.* (ptales)
2. *Herd* is to *cattle* as *pack* is to ___wolves___. (slvewo)
3. *Kangaroo* is to ___mammal___ as *frog* is to *amphibian.* (mlmama)
4. *Sunday* is to *sundae* as *raze* is to ___raise___. (iaers)
5. *Three* is to *nine* as ___twelve___ is to *one-hundred forty-four.* (etvlew)
6. *Blunt* is to ___sharp___ as *bitter* is to *sweet.* (aphrs)
7. ___preheat___ is to *heat* as *impolite* is to *polite.* (tpaeher)
8. *Key* is to *piano* as *string* is to ___guitar___. (itagru)
9. *Squabble* is to ___argue___ as *plummet* is to *fall.* (regua)
10. *Scale* is to *weight* as ___thermometer___ is to *temperature.* (etrtmehmoer)

Try It
Follow the directions to write your own analogies.

1. Write an analogy in which the words are antonyms.
   _____
2. Write an analogy that shows a grammatical relationship.
   _____
3. Write an analo~~Answers will vary.~~
   _____
4. Write an analogy that shows a part-to-whole relationship.
   _____
5. Write an analogy that shows an object-use relationship.
   _____
6. Write an analogy in which the words are synonyms.
   _____

107

Review: Word Roots, Previews and Suffixes, Negatives and Double Negatives

For each suffix or prefix, locate its me~~Answers may vary. Possible answers :~~ing on the first line, and then write an example ~~...~~uffix on the second line.

wrongly	act or process	one who	characterized by or tending to
made of or to make	not or opposite of	again	without

1. -er   one who   baker
2. re-   again   reapply
3. -en   made of or to make   soften
4. -ful   characterized by or tending to   suspenseful
5. mis-   wrongly   mistaken
6. -less   without   penniless
7. -tion   act or process   maturation
8. dis-   not or opposite of   displeased

Each sentence below contains a root or base word with a familiar prefix or suffix. Underline the root or base word and circle the familiar prefix or suffix. (Each root or base word, prefix, and suffix was used in a previous lesson.)

1. Dr. Nelson checks my (respir)ation during my medical exam.
2. Emmanuel hasn't never made a correct (predic)tion about who will win a football game.
3. (Re)formers worked hard to convince the city council to change its mind.
4. A peace(ful) breeze drifted over my face.
5. We were (mis)informed about the starting time and arrived late.
6. Sam sprinkled paprika liberal(ly) onto the casserole.
7. Please don't (inter)rupt the band while they practice.
8. A starfish can (re)generate an arm if one is lost.
9. Spectat(ors) stood in the stands and cheered.

One of the sentences above contains a double negative. Identify the sentence and then rewrite it correctly below.

Emmanuel has never made a correct prediction about who will win a football game.

108

Review: Synonyms and Antonyms, Analogies

Read each word pair. Write **A** on the line if the words are antonyms and write **S** on the line if the words are synonyms.

1. S negotiating bargaining
2. S elderly aged
3. A excitable easy-going
4. S curtains drapery
5. S puzzling clear
6. S confident assured
7. A revealed concealed
8. A disturbed avoided
9. S original unique
10. A agreeable argumentative
11. S anxious jittery
12. S arch curve
13. A segment whole
14. S guard protector
15. A enthusiastic reluctant
16. A honest candid
17. A shanty mansion
18. S secretary assistant
19. A praise ridicule
20. S fence enclosure

Circle the word in parentheses that best completes each analogy.

1. glass : (cup, plate) :: horse : pony
2. gift : wrapping paper :: baby : (rattle, blanket)
3. lamp : (electricity, light) :: hose : water
4. meter : yard :: kilogram : (pound, scale)
5. (the moon, the sun) : Earth :: Jupiter : the sun
6. carving : wood :: (cutting, drawing) : paper
7. solid : liquid :: fall : (plummet, rise)
8. book : library :: (horse, farm) : barn
9. waiter : (restaurant, cook) :: judge : courthouse
10. pinecone : needle :: (acorn, branch) : leaf
11. summer : (beach, swimming) :: winter : skiing
12. deer : herd :: fish : (bunch, school)

Page 109

Homophones are words that sound the same but have different spellings and different meanings. There are hundreds of homophones in the English language.

raised—lifted
razed—tore down

real—actual and true
reel—a cylinder on which material can be wound

gored—pierced or stabbed
gourd—hard-shelled fruit

If you are unsure about which homophone to use, look up the meanings in a dictionary.

Identify It
Circle the correct homophone(s) in each sentence.

1. The child (balled, bald, (bawled)) when her ice cream cone fell to the ground.
2. When Ms. Chan announced the pop quiz, the class let out a ((groan,) grown).
3. The ((yews,) ewes, use) growing alongside our house have gotten much (to, too, two) big.
4. When the ((tide,) tied) goes out, the dock rests on the ground.
5. "The chalice is made of solid 24-(carrot, (karat,) caret) gold," the guide explained.
6. Sofia (lead, (led)) her friends to the backyard (wear, (where)) she ((lets,) let's) her kitten play.
7. Mom ((told,) tolled) me she was not (aloud, (allowed)) to wear ((jeans,) genes) until she was an adult.
8. The Joneses had a skylight installed in the (sealing, (ceiling)) of ((their,) they're, there) living room.
9. Mr. Brown's science class is studying ((cells,) sells) this semester.
10. Tow trucks arrived at the (seen, (scene)) of the accident.
11. On the last page of ((your,) you're) report, be sure to (sight, site, (cite)) the sources you used.
12. Crosby is (do, dew, (due)) for a checkup.
13. The ((soles,) souls) of Candace's (shoos, (shoes)) are quite ((worn,) warn).
14. Next ((week,) weak) the school is ((reseeding,) receding) the ((bare,) bear) spots on the soccer field.

109

Page 110

Proof It
Proofread the following dialogue. It contains multiple errors in homophones. There are 26 mistakes to correct in all.

> ⌐ – deletes incorrect letters, words, punctuation
> ^ – inserts correct letters, words, punctuation

"Hey, Dad," exclaimed Russ, "I've decided what I want to be when I'm done with school."

"That's good news," said Dad. "Have a seat and tell me all about it while you eat your cereal."

"I want to work with dinosaurs," explained Russ. "Well, at least what is left of them. I want to be a paleontologist."

"Don't paleontologists study more than just dinosaurs? I think they also study ancient plants and microorganisms. You need to have your science teacher counsel you on the different areas you could pursue," suggested Dad.

"That's exactly what I plan to do," piped up Russ. "I'm going to meet with the school guidance counselor and discuss the classes I should sign up for next. I also heard there's a paleontologist giving a talk at the museum next week."

"I think you have set a nice course for yourself," continued Dad. "Now, I'm late for the city council meeting. I'll see you later."

Try It
Choose six of the misused homophones that appear in the paragraph above. Write a sentence for each word using the correct meaning.

1. _____
2. _____
3. _____
4. ___ Answers will vary. ___
5. _____
6. _____

110

Page 111

Multiple-meaning words, or **homographs**, are words that are spelled the same but have different pronunciations. They may also sometimes have different meanings.

The word *sow* can mean "to plant seeds" or "a female pig."
Before you sow the [Answers may vary. Possible answers:]
Twelve piglets trotte[d]

Rewrite It
Read each sentence below. Then, write a new sentence using a different meaning for the underlined word. Use a dictionary if you need help.

1. The photographs look best if you let the <u>monitor</u> warm up for an hour or so.
   The scientists will monitor the seal to be sure it is healthy.
2. Be careful when you <u>season</u> the chili; we don't want it to be too spicy.
   Baseball season begins in just three weeks.
3. Mr. McMasters will <u>prune</u> the crabapple trees on Saturday.
   Ms. Lord enjoys dried prunes on her cereal.
4. We are having <u>company</u> stay with us over Labor Day weekend.
   My dad's company is sending him to Taiwan for a month.
5. In the summer, Aunt Flo loves to add a sprig of <u>mint</u> to her iced tea.
   The mint produces millions of coins each year.
6. The stain on Hanna's shirt is so <u>minute</u>, no one will notice.
   It takes only a minute to sign the petition.
7. Dr. Lucas measured the electrical <u>current</u> running through the wire.
   The current edition of the school newsletter is available at the head office.
8. The bridge's steel beams were designed not to <u>buckle</u> under the weight of traffic.
   In the past, a buckle was used instead of a shoestring to tighten a shoe.
9. Kyle's mother is a talented <u>sewer</u> and made all the costumes for the play.
   The rain water washed down into the sewer.
10. We had to buy a <u>permit</u> in order to sell shirts at the concert.
    The grocery store does not permit cats into the store.
11. Ms. Walker attended the council meeting to <u>contest</u> the new budget.
    Lance showed his friends the new glove he won in the contest.

111

Page 112

Solve It
Read each pair of definitions below the word search. Think of the multiple-meaning word that fits both definitions and then find it in the word search puzzle. Words may be written horizontally or vertically, backward, or forward.

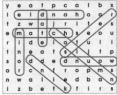

1. younger than 18 years old; less important
   m i n o r
2. category or type; friendly and generous
   k i n d
3. guide or control; bull raised for beef
   s t e e r
4. see romantically; specific day of the month or year
   d a t e
5. part used for carrying or holding; manage or manipulate
   h a n d l e
6. pillar supporting a roof or ceiling; regular section of a newspaper or magazine
   c o l u m n
7. injury; past tense of wind
   w o u n d
8. piece of wood or paper used to start a fire; contest
   m a t c h

112

A word's **denotation** is its actual, literal meaning. It is the meaning you would find if you looked the word up in a dictionary.

A word's **connotation** is the meaning associated with the word. The connotation may be more emotional, or tied to an idea or feeling about the word. Connotations can be positive, negative, or neutral.

For example, the words *skinny, scrawny, slender,* and *slim* all mean approximately the same thing. Their denotation is "not weighing very much; not overweight." The connotation of these words, however, is different. *Scrawny* has a negative connotation—it brings to mind a person or animal that is unhealthy and underweight. *Slender* and *slim* both have a positive connotation—they sound attractive and healthy. *Skinny* can have a positive, negative, or neutral connotation, depending on how it is used.

Identify It
Read each phrase below. On the line, write *positive, negative,* or *neutral,* depending on the connotation of the *italicized* word.

1. a strong *aroma* __positive__
   a strong *odor* __neutral or negative__
   a strong *fragrance* __positive__
   a strong *scent* __neutral or positive__

2. a *sloppy* outfit __negative__
   a *casual* outfit __neutral__

3. the *fragile* display __neutral or positive__
   the *flimsy* display __negative__

4. a *cheap* dinner __negative or neutral__
   an *inexpensive* dinner __neutral or positive__
   a *frugal* dinner __neutral or negative__

5. the *colorful* scarf __neutral or positive__
   the *gaudy* scarf __negative__
   the *vivid* scarf __positive__

   a *fussy* student __negative__
   a *conscientious* student __positive__
   a *meticulous* student __positive__

113

Complete It
Complete each sentence below with a word from the box. The word you choose should have a similar denotation but different connotation from the word in parentheses.

skittish	squandered	lost	pushy
calculated	fussy	glower	exceptional

1. Many people think that Leah has an (odd) __exceptional__ sense of humor.
2. Thomas (spent) __squandered__ his allowance on graphic novels.
3. If you ask her opinion, Jordan will give you a (thoughtful) __calculated__ response.
4. Don't worry about your stuffed bear, Ananya—I'm sure we just (misplaced) __lost__ it.
5. The design of the handbags is quite (detailed) __fussy__.
6. Please try not to (stare) __glower__ at the toddler having a temper tantrum.
7. Although my cousin appears (timid) __skittish__ when you first meet her, she's actually very friendly.
8. If you are (confident) __pushy__ in your beliefs, others will respect your viewpoint.

Try It
Write a sentence for each word below. _Answers may vary._ similar denotations but different connotations. _Possible answers :_

1. nosy __My nosy neighbor is always watching us.__
   inquisitive __An inquisitive mind loves knowing the answer.__
2. unique __The chair has a unique pattern on the seat.__
   bizarre __The house is painted a bizarre color.__
3. hoard __My grandmother likes to hoard junk in her shed.__
   collect __Danni likes to collect old baseball cards.__
4. energetic __The puppy's energetic play was a delight to watch.__
   wild __The monkeys went wild when they saw the man in the yellow hat.__

114

A **simile** is a figure of speech that compares two things using the words *like* or *as.*
The children slept snuggled like puppies on the pile of blankets.
The tiny charm on Ella's necklace was as delicate and perfect as a snowflake.

A **metaphor** is a figure of speech that compares two unlike things that are similar in some way.
The runner's steps were a metronome, thumping a steady beat along the street.
The setting sun was a ball of fire in the dusky sky.

Personification is a figure of speech that gives human characteristics to something that is not human.
The raindrops ran merrily down the window panes.
The cardinal boastfully declared that he had found the prettiest mate in all the town.

Identify It
Read each example of figurative language. On the line, tell what two things are being compared and what figure of speech is used (simile, metaphor, or personification).

1. On the last day of school before summer vacation, Ms. Lottig's class was a zoo.
   __class and zoo; metaphor__

2. Gloria's hurtful words shot like bullets across the room.
   __words and bullets; simile__

3. Alexander knows that an education is the key to his future, which is why he works so hard at school.
   __education and key; metaphor__

4. Nico looked like a sheepdog, peering out from underneath his shaggy bangs.
   __Nico and sheepdog; simile__

5. The wrinkles on Grandma's face were a roadmap to the places her life had taken her.
   __wrinkles and roadmap; metaphor__

6. Silence hung over the room like a heavy veil.
   __Silence and veil; simile__

7. The last tree stood in the empty lot, a soldier awaiting orders.
   __tree and soldier; metaphor__

115

Rewrite It
Rewrite each sentence be[low] _Answers may vary._ personification to make the writing more descriptive or _Possible answers :_ use each type of figure of speech at least once.

1. The icicles hung from the edge of the porch roof.
   __The icicles hung like daggers from edge of the porch roof.__

2. The sun streamed in the windows.
   __The sun threw light through the windows.__

3. The children ran screaming into the playground.
   __The children were wild hyenas screaming across the playground.__

4. Hail bounced against the tin roof for hours.
   __Hail bounced like marbles against the tin roof for hours.__

5. Grace's new moped was shiny and red.
   __Grace's new moped was as shiny and red as a beautiful apple.__

6. The laundry on the line blew in the gentle breeze.
   __The laundry on the line danced in the gentle breeze.__

7. Grandpa Charles was a large man who often wore a stern expression.
   __Grandpa Charles was a bear who often wore a stern expression.__

8. The subway car rumbled into the station.
   __The subway car rumbled into the station like a herd of bulls.__

9. As the deer walked through the woods, leaves crackled underfoot.
   __As the deer walked through the woods, leaves crackled like crumpled paper underfoot.__

10. The flames grew larger as the curtains caught on fire.
    __The flames ate the curtains.__

116

Answer Key

Page 117

Identify It
Underline the ten figures of speech in the following selection.

On Tuesday afternoon, Alejandra and her aunt Sofia packed the trunk of the car and set off on their camping trip. As they eased out of the driveway, the tired old station wagon heaved in protest, but Sofia just grinned and waved good-bye to Alejandra's parents.

"This is going to be so much fun!" exclaimed Alejandra. "I've been looking forward to this trip for ages."

"Me, too," agreed Sofia. "Work has been so stressful lately. But as soon as we got on the road, I felt as free as a bird let out of its cage."

Two hours later, Alejandra and Sofia pulled into the campground and began setting up the tent. "Grrr!" said Sofia, as she struggled with the poles. "This tent is like a puzzle that is missing half the pieces."

Her niece laughed. "No it's not, Aunt Sofia, you're just terrible at following instructions." Alejandra took the crumpled page from her aunt, and in minutes, the dark blue tent stood proudly at attention, happy to welcome them inside.

After a dinner of grilled chicken and corn on the cob, Alejandra and Sofia built a campfire as it began to get dark. The fire cracked and hissed like meat sizzling in a hot pan, and sparks danced and twirled gracefully into the sky.

"Look at that," remarked Sofia, gesturing to the dark blue sky. "The sky is an empty canvas. I'm going to sit right here and watch it fill up with stars." She pulled the woolly blanket around herself until she was wrapped as tightly as a burrito. "That's cozy," she said sleepily. "I could stay here all night."

"I know," said Alejandra, "but I hear my pillow calling for me. I don't think I'll last much longer." She tossed a twig into the fire and stood up, stretching her back. A small movement caught Alejandra's eye, and she peered around the side of the tent. A fat raccoon with eyes gleaming like headlights munched on a discarded corn cob. Alejandra laughed. "Looks like we're not the only ones who enjoy corn for dinner!"

Try It
Describe a place that makes you feel calm and peaceful. Use at least three similes and/or metaphors in your description.

Answers will vary.

117

Page 118

Complete It
Complete each simile below with a word from the box.

hills	wind	gold	baby
feather	mule	bone	honey

1. as sweet as **honey**
2. runs like the **wind**
3. slept like a **baby**
4. as stubborn as a **mule**
5. as old as the **hills**
6. as good as **gold**
7. as light as a **feather**
8. as dry as a **bone**

Try It
On the lines below, write comparisons based

Answers may vary.
Possible answers:

1. Write a metaphor related to music.
   The music of the violins was a bird soaring above the orchestra.

2. Write a simile that includes something related to cooking.
   Our stew bubbled like lava in a volcano.

3. Write a sentence personifying a natural event.
   The tornado grabbed a car and flung it over the field.

4. Write a metaphor about a type of vehicle.
   A motorcycle raced through traffic, a fish darting among crocodiles.

5. Write a simile that includes some type of weather.
   The clouds floated like balloons through the sky.

6. Write a sentence personifying a wild animal.
   A squirrel chattered at the boys, telling them to back off.

7. Write a metaphor about a season.
   Spring finally arrived, a good friend returned from a long vacation.

118

Page 119

Review: Homophones, Multiple-Meaning Words

Read each definition. Choose the correct homophone from the box and write it on the line beside the definition.

dense	stationary	serial	stationery	dents
symbol	muscle	cymbal	mussel	cereal

1. **serial** describes the numbers on a piece of money
2. **cereal** breakfast food eaten with milk
3. **symbol** something that represents something else
4. **cymbal** a percussion instrument made of two metal plates that are clapped together
5. **dense** thick; crowded together
6. **dents** marks or indentations
7. **stationary** standing still; unmoving
8. **stationery** writing paper or materials
9. **mussel** a bivalve sea creature, similar to a clam
10. **muscle** an organ in the body that produces movement

Read each sentence. Then, circle the letter of the definition that describes the meaning of the underlined word as it is used in the sentence.

1. Bryan caught an enormous bass last weekend.
   a. a deep sound   **(b.)** a type of fish
2. The lamp has a manufacturing defect, so I plan to return it.
   (a.) a flaw or imperfection   b. to desert a country
3. Mischa's grandmother has been an invalid for several years.
   (a.) a weak, sickly person   b. not valid, sound, or just
4. Serena Williams was declared the winner of the tennis match.
   a. a thin piece of wood used for starting a fire   **(b.)** a game or contest of skills
5. What's your favorite school subject this year?
   a. to expose to something   **(b.)** topic of study

119

Page 120

Review: Connotations and Denotations, Figures of Speech

Write a sentence using each bold

Answers may vary.
Possible answers:

whether the word, as you used it,   connotation.

1. **unusual** My Uncle Shay has an unusual way of folding clothes.
   neutral
2. **unique** The platypus is a unique animal.
   positive
3. **bizarre** Wow, those are some bizarre pants!
   negative
4. **ambitious** I study mathematics every day because I am ambitious about becoming a scientist. positive
5. **greedy** A greedy troll tried to steal the fairies' riches.
   negative
6. **confident** My daughter is confident that she will do well at the piano recital. neutral
7. **arrogant** Daniel's arrogant attitude caused the judges to grade him on a steeper curve. negative

Each sentence below contains a simile, a metaphor, or personification. Underline each figure of speech, and write **S**, **M**, or **P** on the line to tell what type of figure of speech it is.

1. Steam rose out of Yumi's hot cocoa, leaving a trail behind like a tiny airplane.
   S
2. The crispy bagel eagerly jumped out of the toaster and waited patiently on the counter for Mr. Olivieri to pick her up. **P**
3. Mr. Rozek's stern gaze was a spotlight, making Noah feel uncomfortable and nervous. **M**
4. The kite swooped, ducked, and darted through the air like an excited chickadee. **S**
5. The sunlight was a puddle of gold on the floor of Mei-Ling's bedroom. **M**
6. The scent of hot pancakes and maple bacon beckoned enticingly to Damon from the kitchen. **P**

120
